ROUGH-CUT ELEGIES
AN ANTHOLOGY OF MISSOURI POETS

Edited by Jason Ryberg with special guest
editor, Sharon SingingMoon

Spartan
Press

Spartan Press

Kansas City, MO

spartanpresskc.com

Spartan
Press

Cover image: *Cradling Wheat* by Thomas Hart Benton,
with special thanks to the Saint Louis Art Museum
Title page image: Jason Baldinger
Author photos: T. James Chapman, Edward Ellermann,
Aurora Athelyn, Linda Hays, Carl Neitzert, Nancy Jo Allen,
Shane Epping, Barbara Leonhard, Terry Allen, Kay Palmer.

Acknowledgments:

Nancy Allen: *Dime Show Review.* "Planting Poppies," *I-70 Review:* "Hummingbirds," *MasticadoresUSA:* "Self-Contained-Underwater-Breathing-Apparatice," **Terry Allen:** *Into the Void:* "The Rule of Three," *The Main Street Rag:* "Old Windmill and Shed on Abandoned Farm in Gray and Black," *Still Point Arts and Letters:* "Old Windmill and Shed on Abandoned Farm in Gray and Black"(Reprint), *I-70 Review:* "Aunt Gracie," **Barbara Leonhard:** "Early Spring Snow:" *Spillwords,* "The Found Poems of Amelia Earhart:" *Gorko Gazette Amelia Earhart Anthology,* "Blue Baby:" *Vita Brevis,* **Lynne Jensen Lampe:** "Jitter and Shimmer:" *Isthmus Review,* "Never Stay Where Grief Is Free:" *Anti-Heroin Chic,* **Anand Prahlad:** "Creation;" *Nine Mile Magazine.* **Elijah Burrell:** "Wandering Off," "Reverberations," from *Troubler* (Kelsay Books, 2018), "Heartbreak Neophyte" from *The Skin of the River* (Aldrich Press, 2014), *"Reverberations" from Troubler* (Kelsay Books, 2018); "By This Pond" from *Troubler (*Kelsay Books, 2018),"Postlude / Grace" from *Skies of Blur* (EastOver Press, 2024).

T James Chapman: Special thanks to Jason Ryberg and Spartan for giving me a shot and keeping rock n roll on the jukebox. John Dorsey for all the help and for putting up with me all the way to Lawrence. Lesley Day, Dan Wright, Kyle & Bobby, Goodiehouse, the Re:Born crew, Brett Underwood, Mic B, and A Moment Zine for keeping St. Louis Poetry strong. My grandma for raising me, and Angel for tolerating me.

Aurora Athelyn: Special thanks to Kate Watt, Glenn Irwin, Shane Seely, Kelly Stolle, Melody Walkenhorst, Jenn Potts, Hannah Rowland, and Katie from the Motel 60 in Winona.

Table of Contents

Aurora Athelyn

Flossie's Apple Barrel / 1

Blazing Star / 4

Rebuilding / 6

Night Paddle / 7

Dandelion / 8

Colorado - Kansas Border / 9

A Sestina for Self-Sovereignty / 10

Limestone Calamint / 12

valvoline / 13

The Four Seasons on Lāna'i / 15

T. James Chapman

A Little Flair / 19

Old Time Music and Sacred Songs / 20

Spook House / 21

Last Night's Square Dance / 22

Warrant Checks and Evil Living / 23

Roaches like the Rest of Us / 24

Shout at the Devil / 25

I Got A Bone to Pick with Tammy Wynette / 26

Road Songs / 27

Me and Jesus / 28

Ben Kuzemka

I am writing this with the assumption / 31

Madelyn died on an ATV in Lincoln County. / 32

On the ninth day the lord said / 35

I stand beside you / 37

It is the year of cicadas; I am no longer a poet. / 38

It's midnight, there's meatless lasagna / 39

Let's finish this Lacroix and watch

   the rideshares draw near / 40

We moved to this place / 41

How new we've become / 43

A ceiling fan, discount fluorescent / 44

Nancy Jo Allen

Planting Poppies / 47

Hummingbirds / 48

Fishing from the Dock / 50

S.O.S. / 52

The Day She was Born / 53

Self-Contained Underwater Breathing Apparatus / 54

You Float with Ease / 56

As Delicate as Paper / 57

Goldfinch / 59

Becoming / 60

Walter Bargen

Remaining Remote / 63

Trumpets of Jericho / 64

Secular Circularity / 65

When the Other Shoe Drops / 67

One Sixty-Fourth of Everything / 68

Porched / 70

Out the Window / 71

Home Crucifixion 1 / 72

Home Crucifixion 2 / 73

Seven Seas / 74

Terry Allen

The Rule of Three / 79

Old Windmill and Shed on Abandoned Farm
    in Gray and Black / 81

Waiting on the Last Train / 84

About the Light / 86

Flying Squirrels Can't Really Fly / 88

Aunt Gracie / 90

Folktales in the Dark / 91

My Aunt and Uncle Drop By Our House
    for a Visit in the 1950s / 94

"And May God Bless You… You Jerk!" / 97

The Old Man Schmoozes with the Guy Who
    Owns a Bar around the Corner / 100

Barbara Harris Leonhard

Surfing the White 'Cats': A Kayaker's Tale / 105

To My Knees, Whom I Named Tina and Cher / 107

Aunt Rona Visits: I Forget to Mask / 109

Early Spring Snow / 110

Ophelia / 111

The Lost Child / 112

The Found Poems of Amelia Earhart / 114

Blue Baby / 115

His Mourning Heart / 117

This, a River / 118

Lynne Jensen Lampe

Jitter and Shimmer / 123

No Sleep Is Safe in a Cold Bed / 125

How to Change a Pillowcase / 126

When Light Gardens for Truth / 128

Never Stay Where Grief Is Free / 129

When Light Calls the City Home / 132

Love Language / 133

Fat Quarters / 135

Rough-Cut Elegy / 137

When Light Unlocks the Cellar of Time / 39

Elijah Burrell

Dreamers and Drifters / 143

Wandering Off / 144

Favored / 145

Heartbreak Neophyte / 146

Where Have You Been / 148

Reverberations / 149

When He Types Her Name It
    Autocorrects to Distant / 150

By This Pond / 151

Diver\Down / 152

Postlude / Grace / 153

Anand Prahlad

Twilight in Hanover County, 1965 / 157

Shells / 158

sister / 160

Creation / 162

Mana / 164

The Cows / 166

Helium / 168

Remembering San Francisco / 170

Adrift / 172

Patching / 175

Introduction

Thomas Gray said, "Poetry is thoughts that breathe and words that burn." Others may say that poets are Dreamers and Drifters living among their imaginings that Jitter and Shimmer. Some consider poetry to be the Helium of human Creation, allowing us to rise like the voices singing Old Time Music and Sacred Songs in unison. Whatever brought you to this anthology, we welcome you to experience the thoughts expressed in the words of these ten Missouri poets.

It has been a joy to sample the variety and breadth of talent represented here. Poetry allows each writer a vehicle of self-expression, allows the reader a window into the poet's sensibilities. Whether an expression of joy as in Barbara Leonhard's poem, *Early Spring Snow*, "still, the birds will sing.....as though they are free". Or Anand Prahlad's self-reflection in *Mana*, "I am myself the dance of no movement/ sunrise on the desert", poetry has a way of calling us to ourselves.

Poets ask uncomfortable questions, make statements of truth we may wish to ignore as Aurora Athelyn does in her poem *The Four Seasons* on Lana'i – "CATTLE XING sign hangs obsolete, reminding the island what happens to invasive species." Terry Allen reflects on his brother's transition to assisted living in *Flying Squirrels Can't Really Fly*, "His memories thin fragments of torn fabric".

Then there are the reminiscent ramblings of Ben Kuzemka, as he lays his thoughts of Madelyn "who would have killed Kobe to be Kobe" on the page. And Nancy Jo Allen's

expression of loss in her poem, *The Day She Was Born*, "…
she survived, but is now separated from me without a life
line". Walter Bargen, Missouri's first poet laureate proclaims,
"in the house of words, your tongue is a hammer" in his
poem, *Home Crucifixion #1*.

In *Rough-Cut Elegies*, my fellow Missouri poets have
shared their hearts, their souls and this anthology invites
you into their worlds. I guarantee you will find a poem
you love, a poet you want to hear more from and a deep
appreciation of the poets of Missouri. Thank you, Jason
Ryberg and Spartan Press. It has been an honor.

-Sharon SingingMoon

I hope my story don't make you cry
But this birdie flew too high;
He flew from his old Missouri home
He fell right into the city ways, like dancin' in cabarets
From party to party he would roam…

Poor little robin walkin', walkin', walkin' to Missouri;
He can't afford to fly
Got a penny for a poor little robin, walkin', walkin',
    walkin' to Missouri;
Got a teardrop in his eye.

-Sammy Kaye, *Walkin' to Missouri*

Aurora Athelyn

Aurora Athelyn is a hiker and writer from Missouri. During a 2023 thru-hike of the Ozark Trail, she stuck out her thumb for a food resupply in Van Buren, MO. A silver minivan stopped and whisked her away to Main Street Market. The driver introduced herself as Athelyn and spoke highly of her own minivan. Aurora bonded with Athelyn on the car ride to the trailhead. Athelyn was kind enough to offer her name to Aurora's first born. Knowing she will never have children, Aurora chose it for her new surname. Aurora's poetry has previously appeared under the name Aurora Blanchard in the following literary journals: *Litmag 2021*, *Litmag 2023*, and the *Arkansas Review*. She is currently a teaching assistant and English graduate student at the University of Missouri - St. Louis.

Flossie's Apple Barrel

While Flossie writes our drink orders in pen,
The man at our table with gout calls out
"Bacca" to the man sitting to my left
And let's just say he's named after
Chewbacca because that simplifies things
But Flossie says she would like vodka too
And I can tell from her gravelly laugh
She's hit her quota of Newports today
But if I were in Flossie's shoes
I'd hear the name "Bacca" as "vodka" too
And I think Gout Man liked Flossie confused

And I still haven't wrapped my head around
What type of restaurant this is because it's
Not quite Southern, not quite Appalachian,
Not quite Midwestern. Maybe Ozarkan
In the wake of Scots-Irish immigrants
And abandoned mining operations
But anyway, Flossie's new fish special
Comes with mushrooms, hush puppies, and french fries
But I order fried liver and okra
And Flossie's eyes light up; she might have guessed
I'm an out-of-towner in demeanor

And when I fidget, the tablecloth sticks
To my wrists like duct tape and my friend Kat
Asks if I want to play musical chairs
And it's a no, but she doesn't listen
And gets up anyway to stand between

Me and lavish rivers of cigarette
Ingredients: benzene, tar, and menthol
Right through her shirt sleeves 'til Flossie returns
With our brown plates of food and I wonder
If she resents serving tourists here
When Rocky Falls Shut-Ins is *right there*

A 15-minute drive she'll never make
Anyway on a day off she won't take
But if she does, it will be for laundry
And babysitting her grandkids in A/C
Feeding them Dollar General applesauce
And soothing their cries with plastic models
Taking care of everyone, trying to
Take care of me when I start to feel queasy
And says she can take the liver off
My tab because it's not my cup of tea
(Nicely) but it's gone rancid in deep freeze

And even though our water's not been filled,
The wood panels are a live museum
Advertising five-cent Ebbert apples
From Kentucky and a bag of charcoal
From Greer Spring, circa 1965
And a blond kid crying in cowboy chaps
For the *Saturday Evening Post*
And it distracts me from the corner booth
Building up mountains of bloody napkins
Marooned by the slip of a dull steak knife.
With bated breath my lungs swell, trapping smoke

From the Diet Coke lady's cigarette
One table away; she flicks dying ash
Into the tray and leans on her hooked cane
And leaves a crumpled bill behind the band
Of Bluegrass musicians wearing denim
And my friend looks sideways at the cash drawer
Framed in red lattice, saying we should pay
While we still can, but, really, it's practice
For her self-restraint because she's been trained
In first aid and keeps gauze in the Chevy
But in here it's Flossie who runs the game.

Blazing Star

(Liatris Spicata)

Slouching up the sun-soaked ridge,
Padded by bleached grass,
Haunted by fading tendrils of purple coneflower,
Liatris, self-named, carries a chainsaw,
Weighed down by orange chaps,
Protected hip to calf.

Armored in linen and Carharts
Wisps of hair escape her construction helmet
Giving gray to the Godsend wind.

Here and there, green and white signs
Steady the mind.
Wayward hikers find the path most traveled
Ghosting the overgrown trail behind.

Liatris the plant cures snake bites when mashed up
Regulating cycles of irregular bleeding,
Soothing sandpaper throats,
Bottle brushing the kidneys, bladders, and ovaries.
Liatris the human stalks fallen trees and performs surgery
Shaving the innards, spilling fresh guts of sawdust—
    bile, relief!

Fuschia veins dapple the igneous glades.
Liatris backtracks and hangs a green and white sign—

A beacon on the Ozark Trail—when the path is unclear.
Back at camp under the safety of a whip-poor-will
    canopy
Sipping fermented tea after trail maintenance
Liatris heats up her own ratatouille on a tin stove
Takes off her hat and mumbles she should have moved
    away from Kansas
At night, the antennae in her tent transmits camaraderie
…Cardinals bat and field another victory

The flower, Liatris, also known as
Button Snakeroot or Thickspike Gayfeather,
Sways on the prairie glade
Ferrying salt-sealed rumors to the grave.

Rebuilding

Brimstone burns   barricades of faith,
Bottling blood   and bruised indignation.
I round up remnants   of singed rock
Stacking stones   for a lone shelter,
Whittling away   winter days,
Naked to the wind's   numb whisper.
I collect courage   to coax a hearth.
The embers embolden   my entreaty in
Feeble fury,   until a fawn
Prances in, ferrying   parcels of friendship.

Night Paddle

I follow the current back home
Skimming my fingers across the river
Leaving in their wake
Rivulets splintering glass
Sending foam shoreside to the oracle

The prophecy of the past bobs in the waves
Back to me. I place the oar at an angle, holding fast
To veer into a lazy cove for a beat, massaging my
    worn shoulder
At a bend in the river at the hospital
Where my soul entered the world blizzard-born

My mom said when I came out of the womb
I shrieked to the world that I was here and alive
Looking back, I think that should have been a sign
That I did not want to leave that warm amniotic fluid
Did not want to paddle upstream all my life

Tipping, shifting my weight toward the moon's runny
    reflection
Falling in. Left foot. Right foot. My big toe
Fingers the muddy river bottom, hooked
To silt, held by its womb until an old
Catfish nudges my foot out of his home.

Dandelion

As a child I met the dandelion—
A kindred misfit in a grassy field—the only spot of yellow!
She glows like the belt loops of Orion,
But most dads treat her like a stray hair in Jell-O!

In second grade I used the flower to imprint
Mustard stars on gifted napkins, to reassure
My favorite teacher: all you have to do is squint—
See a piece of art, make it your tincture.

A hundred years ago she fit neatly in a tonic
Soothing the liver, kidney, and gallbladder—
But! If brewed by a witch, she was labeled demonic,
Crushed in the cabinet next to the Jacob's Ladder.

I never believed the adults who called the dandelion a weed
And my suspicion was confirmed—it's groundcover!
If only she'd been introduced by the likes of Johnny
    Appleseed—
Perhaps then, maybe middle-aged men would love her...

Colorado - Kansas Border

Stars outside the church van window
Dimmed in the hotel parking lot—
Zeus wagged his bushy tail on the mildew carpet
As the answering machine flashed

I waited in the Motel 8 for dinner
Flipping channels with a chewed
Remote, settling on a movie I'd never
Seen—Karate Kid III

My stepmom came in,
Keys jangling, and my sister's
Mood darkened
As Zeus licked her Gameboy

I heard the steak was rubber
But I didn't know enough about it—
My hands grew sticky
Playing with the ketchup from Applebee's

Out of boredom, I skimmed a Bible
From the nightstand drawer for two days

Until my dad could walk in a pink gown
"Giardia free" and we drove back to Missouri

A Sestina for Self-Sovereignty

It won't be mortgage
It won't be marriage
It won't be motherhood
That ties down this body
And for every suitcase packed, the latch
Dangles open behind me, womanly

And the shape of the road is womanly
And you bet I will mortgage
My life in exchange for transience and won't latch
Onto marriage
Hanging onto my body
Which, through lust, could accidentally yield motherhood

In every partner, there is motherhood
Siphoning womanly
Comfort out of a body
Dancing with pincers around mortgages
In a playpen marriage
Teasing the cold rim of that sliding latch

I hatch an escape plan in case the latch
Ever closes in on motherhood,
Ever threatens marriage
Ever calls on womanly
Principles that would warrant a mortgage
Over my own body

As if I have to pay for my own body
As if I don't own it outright, as if the latch
Locks us into a mortgage.
Meanwhile, self-motherhood
Unlocks some womanly
Semblance of a Boston marriage

Because what is marriage
If not a stake in the body,
Tied to some person, place, or womanly
Thing that could free the latch
From someone else's motherhood,
Someone else's mortgage

In marriage I would mortgage
My body in unwomanly
Self-motherhood, latching onto sovereignty

Limestone Calamint

(Clinopodium arkansanum)

Butterfly wings thrum back and forth between
Purple bottlebrush flowers swaying gently in the breeze
Atop igneous rock glades I would mistake for blacktop
If I weren't three days deep in the backcountry

Buoyed by the humans I'd seen earlier climbing the bluffs
Above the Eleven Point River but after a few minutes
    of chit-chat
I had scampered off
Not putting myself in the way of their company

Climbing up, up, up to the land of leaping ticks and orange
    pine needles
Sweltering under the July heat in my bug net
I pulled off ticks—no, not ticks but new freckles made
    by the sun?—
Camouflage. Deception.

I need to study my new spots.
I sit down to rest on more igneous rock and smell
    chocomint—but not!
Wafting from a spindly wisteria-colored flower so delicate
I could snap the stem between my thumb and index finger

I know I'll forget to look up the species
When I can return to the long aisles of freezers
Stocking Mediterranean Mint gelato
Far from the Mediterranean, far from the Ozarks.

valvoline

bored,
tired—but
guy
named
Jay
at
the oil
change place
gave me
new life
after
my
dipstick
dried
in
quarantine—
what a funny
desperate
feeling
to flip my
hair
through the
window
just to say
hey I am
very
available

for one
night—
Valentine's Day—
but he smiled and
waved
me out of the garage,
professionally

The Four Seasons on Lāna'i

The spirits appear by night, in the hotel garden.

They are taro and ube.

They are clouds of dust, fishermen, bleached coral,
Mormon landowners,

And shreds of plastic tarp silhouetting the bygone
plantation era.

The orange cat is stoic, a favorite in the crowd

Of Birkin bags and aloha shirts.

They watch the stray cat track

Orbs of light

Blinking in circles around the pink petals

Of endangered awikiwiki plants

(Canavalia pubescens)

The spirits float to the suite, twist the blinds, finger the
remote,

And make a racket in the vents. Pearl white upholstery

Travels to the dump once a season, collecting

Molecules of feces from the axis deer population

Outnumbering the island residents.

The horses chew alfalfa and earn Larry Ellison

Millions. The *CATTLE XING* sign

Hangs obsolete, reminding the island

What happens to invasive species

T. James Chapman

T. James Chapman is a worker and poet from Southeast Missouri. He'll buy you a beer and tell you how good the cornbread is at St. Louis City Jail. Holler at him to grab his new chapbook HOLY THE HALE BOPP APOCALYPSE: tylertchapman@gmail.com

A Little Flair

What am I without amphetamines?
What is Marty Robbins without a trumpet?
I reckon a damn good songwriter still, but
lacking a little flair.

Tom T. Hall wrote *Harper Valley PTA*. He
sang it in a living room with an acoustic guitar,
weren't no drums or horns or harmonies.
Now, Jeannie C. Riley is a hell of a singer,
but, I like Tom's version.

Most folks don't seem to feel that way,
so give me some
Jeannie C. Riley on a foil, or a trumpet line
chopped out on a CD case:

Marty Robbins' Greatest Hits of course.
They all had a little flair.

Old Time Music and Sacred Songs

Music ain't a thread, but a long chain
at least 3/8" - at least
a bike lock is too easily cut, a thread snaps

maybe music is an anchor chain
the kind strongmen dragged on television
when I was a kid
a chain to plunge the depths

folks you don't know and never will
you do now.
they are kin.
familiar faces.

his grandpa a century back had a favorite sacred song
your great grandma a couple decades back did too
O COME, ANGEL BAND and help me lug
this miles long chain
a burden I'm happy to bear

Spook House

I learned punk rock from a preacher man
learned bluegrass from a junkie
learned drinkin' from my daddy
and hard work from my grandma

There's nothing you can't learn with eyes
peeled like grapes in a low-budget haunted house

where I'm from all the spook houses are
built to scare crooked kids straight
back to the arms of the lord
away from their drinkin' daddies
and the hell of petty walmart theft
or the heaven of velvet paintings
of elvis
of card-shark dogs
of topless women
and overdoses on fun
or heroin
or budweiser 2 by 4's

St. Francois County Jail is still
called the Terrordome
and you'll find out why if you spend the night.
don't make a pallet there.

take heed the haunted house!
take heed the church house spooks!
take heed your grandma and the preacher man!
just don't become a square.

Last Night's Square Dance

I broke quite a sweat circling my corner
light as a feather,
my stiff-as-a-board demeanor broke too
and I cracked a smile with strangers
for the first time in a while

I've heard the most rugged among us,
hay tossin' men, weep as they broke
into purple monologues praising
the square dance for chopping
their boundaries down to stumps

somewhere after twirling my partner
and circling to the right, the caller called
we ain't got all night
and I wished we did. I was out of breath
and out of any clue as to where
I'd rather be than last night's square dance

Warrant Checks and Evil Living

like cowboy boots on packed snow
I've slid through life, I've busted my ass
and I love the way the bruises look
after a week or so, wise and yellowed

I thrive on acceleration
and accelerants
I seek turbulence and rip
through it like a tugboat

my pops pulled a jacked up truck out of a ditch
with a '94 Chrystler LeBaron
I need to pull more poems out of my ass
and may need to catch a felony for inspiration

but

I'm too scared to check CaseNet

Roaches like the Rest of Us

Cop cars creep down side streets
roaches like the rest of us
thankful the streetlights don't shine

god's size-12 could stomp us out
any time.
any where.
twice on sunday.

his thick soles respect no man
some of us beg on our knees
for more discipline
the less fortunate among us
are stomped out early.

friends scatter under the fridge and soon,
start dreaming of their next meal
the rest of us keep busy
dodging our two-stepping christ

hard to smell the roses,
we barely got time to smell the Raid

omnipresent size-12 from heaven!
let us stroll without a care
the tint of our glasses don't mean much
when our eyes are bulging.

Shout at the Devil

the record spins backward
spewing satanic messages our parents
knew were on them
they were right to break them
to burn the covers and smoke inside the house

a toddler curses Busch beer as swill
half-empty can, warm,
next to a filled ash tray
all he cares about is christmas anyway

santa ain't quite as fat as dad gets,
decades after his records got spint backwards
he was right to spray paint pentagrams in the street
to break dance and smoke outside the school

a teen praises Busch beer as cheap
quarter-full can, warm,
used as a cupholder ashtray
all he cares about is halloween anyway

I Got A Bone to Pick with Tammy Wynette

the patroness saint of country music
gave Grandma direct orders
and by god
Grandma followed them

from being crowned Basketball Queen
at Elvins High, all the way to
pawpaw's rotten brain and frail body
convulsing for the last time,
she never disobeyed those orders
handed down to her from
the radio waves
and wavy 45RPM records

Road Songs

for David Nemerov

we've turned homeless and hungry
into van life and fasting
stroked the horns of bulls
and cupped life's balls

we've churched up our menial jobs:
it's just keeping our work honest

our bosses wouldn't piss in our mouths
if our teeth was on fire
but we're parched and dying
so we drink life and cal it living

Me and Jesus

Me and Jesus Christ
we got a bone to pick
with you Mr. Megachurch Pastor
your First Lady too

How we gonna feed five thousand
when you bought up all the farmland?
You leveled the trees but wanna go hunting
hunting for converts

but consider my trees painted Posted Purple
cause the only one who prospers
off the prosperity gospel
is you

Ben Kuzemka

Ben Kuzemka grew up in suburban Chicago and now lives in suburban Saint Louis with his spouse and two young kids. His collection *Dance Grooves for Gotikara* was published by Spartan Press in 2018.

1

I am writing this with the assumption
that you will soon be gone,
that slightly less soon I will drive
to our old suburb in the rain
and see one or two old friends for froyo and kebab.

I wouldn't have recognized you at the supermarket,
but I will recognize you that day. I'll tell your holy father so.
I believe you named your cat 'F Scott'
and never got over that barista with the Dashboard tattoo.

I will think of you on the way
as morning staggers on, and I blink away the counties
    named for generals,
bankers, and communists. But I won't think of you
    on the way home.

I'll picture work and laundry, and taste
the melting cold brew and the fading shawarma.

I will not send this, but I feel you'll receive it tonight
    despite my tact,
and I'll soon see more photos of ugly, fat, frantic
    little F Scott.
To you now I say into the tile
the only words I've ever learned to say.

2

Madelyn died on an ATV in Lincoln County.
She went to school with real life nuns and sat
in their offices with her mother

and no one understood Kandinsky like her,
or Bukowski, or Barefoot wine mixed
with vodka, or Maxo Kream.

Madelyn could do jumping jacks
in her bathrobe and could hate her own laughter.

And she learned to ski at seven
and learned Mussorgsky at eight
and quit violin at thirteen
and quit lacrosse at fourteen
because she learned
at Breckenridge
that freedom is summit and negation.

Her mixed media is showing in Jefferson County
        and I'm there
for a second time
in the square that smells of
gunpowder.

For a morning I'm back in Laos
surrounded by motorcycles, jungle, Australians.
Surrounded by fresh clove cigarettes and papaya
and rocket launchers ripping into the jungle

and a swirl of languages and youth
and like Wilde she worshipped youth
and Ruskin
and unlike Wilde
she died
young.

It is late winter and I've heard there are Belorussians
    dying en route
to a bus in Alaska, and Madelyn died on an atv in
    Lincoln County
and she knows I'm here
holding her hair back
and she knows you're here too, trying
with us
to give a shit,
hand-in-hand,
very far
away from such empty places.   .

-

Madelyn would've killed Kobe to be Kobe,
but she died closer to void than Kobe.
And her sister cried but remembered how
Madelyn was always too pretty without trying,
and her brother cried but remembered
how his inheritance just increased
and maybe he'll name his second daughter Madelyn,
but only her middle name,
and he'll spell it properly.

And her parents will miss her laughter
but not the sound of
her muffler past midnight, but shit,
dammit, Madelyn was the sound of her muffler
    past midnight—
the German electric sputtering of dissolve
and neglect and power and anger—
the quiet surge
of an engine sleeping
in a large front lawn.

There are folks falling into the Ganges taking selfies
and one dude got ate by a lion or some shit
and some teens got beheaded in Morocco
and their friends at home liked vodka and Monster
and Madelyn died on an ATV in Lincoln County,
or rather she was violently thrown from an ATV in
    Lincoln County
and landed in several pieces on top of Lincoln County
and the friends vomited and sped away.

The nuns pray for her, and maybe I do too.
I see her mixed media in this cheap museum,
in between exhibits of local teens
still creating
and a landscapist who dies next June.

3

On the ninth day the lord said
nothing is ever done.

The snow now melting is mine
and so my daughter it is yours

and with it we will paint
planets anew.

On the ninth day Borges
regained his sight

and lit his last candle
in the thunder of the cape.

On the ninth day
dusty-eyed children stood in line
and waited for a promise

parents had once whispered of,
a promise not shared in years—

a word which when thawed could reflect
the cool light of a forgotten day.

The children laughed
and speculated because the only path
before them was providence

and no providence is complete
without something like
anticipation.

On the ninth day the water
receded to the dam
and crawled into the reservoir

and on the shore
I saw a face

I once knew
still, waiting
just to tell me

let's go.

4

I stand beside you
there
between the light
of the screen
and the air.

I'm of the opinion that we share
many thoughts

I have seen the way
you trim your bangs,
the sites you use
for reviews,
the Joni songs
we both cling to.
We are the same,

and erupting silk
between us
is daylight thunder
which indeed does twist
us and changes
our nitrogen
but not our need for nitrogen,
not here—
not in bubble-shaped sky.

5

It is the year of cicadas; I am no longer a poet.
I don't like the Rolling Stones or hamburgers at midnight.

I hear cicadas instead of my wash machine.
When their groans crescend into this room
I think either of midcap value or the mercy of Christ.

I write my daughter's name in green ink,
in fine ink, in templates and forms and those
dots which hide passcodes so well.

I'm reminded of what Marlowe once wrote about
   veganism—
about what we said
once jetting our souls atop the maroon bay twenty nine
   years ago next year,
with calms and magnolia in our hair.

6

It's midnight, there's meatless lasagna
in the oven. How are you?

I remember something I once read about Neptune—
how it is blue, rather large, kinda gassy.
I remember driving back north
one Americano at a time.

Time, you once said, has a name, a way of referring
     to herself.
A trucker handle, of sort. It's doxa won't change
when the oven beeps and the fake cheese glistens.

At least we are not alone
and breathe no air alone.
These are the lunging sands. I see, I see.

7

Let's finish this Lacroix and watch the rideshares draw near.
It's warm on this floor—a Wednesday twilight,
Bremen/Lausanne from the unlit hallway.
Let's ask to have the windows down. My hair doesn't
    move these days, but let's have the windows down.

There is a park, and it'll be near dark when we get there;
let's take photographs.
I'm too tired to be entertained, and I know you are too.
You talk in your sleep now, just like me.

I admit to being moved by this idea, this almost-memory.
I think in decent faith

this asphalted thing, this urge
to escape
is providence in disguise.

8

We moved to this place
in the year of cicadas.

We rented men and trucks and drove
west into sunlit hills.

This is now my wood.
At night they turn the color of meconium.

I have composite plans on my Japanese desk
of what I will do to them—
how I will shape them, raze them,
make them likeable and new.

The oaks make me wheeze and sneeze,
and they are where my good daughter will come to know

the shapes of the forgiving stars
the weight of tennis racquets, chalk brushes, the musk
    of glitter.

We moved to this place
because it was here and we could.
I take less walks now
but I am told they are better walks.

It was here, and I could reach
out and grab the dirt from this planet

which is mostly dirt-covered copays and airports.

It is here, and only the planet can make it go away,
which it will, when the streetlight melts into the stream.

9

How new we've become
at this, the end of an ice age.

The company which makes my headphones is in the news.
Bitcoin just hit fifty. You once told me it'd be so.
In my occasional dreams
you become the prophet you claimed to be.

For my part, I often listen to Elvis.
I push buttons for coffee and cake.
Sometimes I feel the tender
center in my arms
when I dance unalone to Let it Be or help
my daughter climb the stairs.
I am here shaped as halasana to wait
for melody to rise from the dissonance.

10

A ceiling fan, discount fluorescent
bulbs. We are the magi,
the eight of us, the horde of us.

And we are here at last
to ask for the asking words.

Something delicate is now with us and beyond us
for this is the place of dreams

and we the children of dreams
ignored and cherished in that order—
dreams nurtured to lovely, obsolete birth.

I believe every action has an effect
and I sense that you are my friend

so remind me once more
why we began, and what
beginning said.

Nancy Jo Allen

Nancy Jo Allen lives in Columbia, Missouri. Her poetry collections, *Wrinkles in Time and in Love,* and *Wild and Tame* are available through Kelsay Books and Amazon. Her third collection, *Darkness and Light*, will be released in the summer of 2024, and available through the same vendors.

Planting Poppies

I open a mouth
in the early morning earth,
and remove a bedding
plant with care
from its fragile,
plastic container
that protects roots
as tangled as veins
that feed human
bodies. I ponder opioids
that this beautiful plant
provides to terminal
patients. The plant
grows in fields
soaking in sun rays
like bodies on beaches
converting sunshine
to something useful;
narcotics act upon networks
of nerves, quieting pain
screaming for attention.
My hands close soil
in place and Gaia
swallows roots. I
think of Mother's lips
closing around that last pill
pressed under her tongue.

Hummingbirds

On the dusty window sill,
early evening sunlight
deepens the pastel colors
painted on porcelain pinions
spread open in flight. Father
collected figurines
of finely featured hummingbirds.
He hung red sugary feeders
near a window in his summer home
where tiny flitting birds
fed with quick movements
in and out to sip, maneuvering
with the skill of dogfighters.
It seemed so effortless to his eye
as wings beat too rapidly to detect.
When nesting began, father
watched as the females
employed beaks, chests and rumps
pushing moss, lichen, twigs,
leaves, even dryer lint
into demitasse shape with spider's
sticky webbing. They built them
camouflaged in high altitudes
as snug as his tail gunner
seat in the B-17 that carried him
humming high above Europe
to bomb bridges,

ammunition dumps,
railroads, and battle fields.
Did he think of the parachute silk
strapped to his back
as wings to escape when bombs
burst the fuselage?

Fishing from the Dock

At first, my feet
did not touch the waves
under the dock
unless I was seated near the beach sands.
As my legs grew,
they dangled in the water.
I observed the baiting and catching,
and scales of red-breasted sunnies
and silver crappies flash in the sun.

Silver, red, blue, green, yellow—all lovely.

Then, I had a pole with a line,
a sinker, a hook—
I learned to bait with conscripted worms—
and a red and white bobber
that disappeared when a fish took the bait.
The water was shallow,
greenish-yellow and sometimes frothy
beneath a blue sky.
The waves moved with the rhythm
of the world's rotation and gravity
while I waited for the tug to arrive.

I learned by fishing,
that flash attracts,
but one can be caught,

descaled,

gutted,

filleted

and served for dinner

if one takes the dangled bait.

S.O.S.

Eternal vigilance is the price of liberty—
John Philpot Curran, 1790

High above Vancouver Island
gliding the drafts
over Quatsino Sound where land
splits forming brackish waterways,
a bald eagle plunges
sinking talons
into an octopus
whose tentacles
wrap round its feathered body.
It chirrups
and whistles weakly
splashing to not drown
as it would have if not for a few
Canadian salmon farmers
who struggle to set it free
rather than let nature play out.
So, its majesty survives
the corrupting prehensile
grasp of an invertebrate.

The Day She was Born

I sat upon the deck
amid the tree tops
on a May evening three weeks
past her due date and cried.
I went to bed and relaxed.
The first pangs—
strong, close, dilated to eight,
and too late for an epidural.
Born blue and strangling
on her own life line,
the team fought to revive her
and she survived,
but is now separated
from me without a life line.

Self-Contained Underwater Breathing Apparatus

I learned about buoyancy
and weighted belts.
The belt had spaces to add
one pound at a time that kept me submerged
where I learned how to navigate depths.
At first, it was in a pool—
starting in the shallows,
heading for the deep end.
Weeks passed.
There were manageable calculations
to estimate how much time and air
I had available to sustain life.
Then came the outdoor test
in a body of water provided by nature.
I had to gear up,
properly flip overboard
into the dark water of the lake.
I swam to the bottom—
about twenty-feet below—
where I ditched my SCUBA tank,
took a deep breath of compressed air,
turned off the valve,
and slowly ascended,
letting the air in my lungs expand
and bubble out through my opened mouth.
On the surface I gulped air
and descended to the bottom
as the air compressed.

In the dark depths, I reached for my diving regulator,
turned on the valve, took a breath,
slipped on the tank, secured it in place
and rose to the surface like a phoenix.

That certification test prepared me for divorce.
Life continued after ditching what restricted my air.
I surfaced, but I left *that* tank behind,
and began to breath air without being weighted down.

You Float with Ease

through the stream of life
like a salmon in the shallows,
sun glinting on your silver scales,
whereas,
I fight my way upstream
against violent currents and rapids,
evading predators
all to leave eggs to be fertilized,
and start a new generation,
so I can die.

As Delicate as Paper

-after Pat Brentano's *Missing Birds*

tears under pressure—
fragile as thin bird shells
too frail to incubate offspring.
Tree canopies disappearing
in which to nest.
Fire,
fire,
yet more fire.
Clear cutting for crops,
for human habitats
much too large
to share with nature.
Ground nesters homes
exchanged for foundations
and basements.
Fish feeding birds
poisoned by secondary kill
where water is scarce
and thickening
into sludge.
Soil—
climate dried—
that does not sustain
worms for robins,
with disappearing vegetation
for seed consumption.

Confined to limited spaces,

they compete in hunger games.

Chopped to pieces off runways—

once safe causeways.

Delicately balanced in squares of paper

hung from the ceiling above us.

Their songs gone.

Their unique beauty

in a unique environment gone,

reduced to an empty space,

torn from nature under pressure

as delicate as paper.

Goldfinch

A goldfinch plucks seeds
from a cone flower—
just yesterday pink and brown.
Drought has dried the plants
as though it were September,
but recent rains restored green,
plush foliage.
The bird moves on.

Becoming

A diary rests on the mantle
near my chair.
It is a gift
from my husband
who encourages my writing.
Its leather binding
and covers are lovely—
both supple and strong—
a bit like my writing
has become.

Walter Bargen

Walter Bargen has published 27 books of poetry including: *My Other Mother's Red Mercedes* (Lamar University Press, 2018), *Until Next Time* (Singing Bone Press, 2019), *Pole Dancing in the Night Club of God* (Red Mountain Press, 2020), *You Wounded Miracle,* (Liliom Verlag, 2021), *Too Late to Turn Back* (Singing Bone Press, 2023), and *Radiation Diary: Return to the Sea* (Lamar University Press, 2023). He was appointed the first poet laureate of Missouri (2008-2009). His awards include: a National Endowment for the Arts Fellowship, Chester H. Jones Foundation Award, and the William Rockhill Nelson Award. He currently lives outside Ashland, Missouri, with his wife and too many formerly feral cats.

Remaining Remote

How many televisions were shot today?
How many televisions stepped on land mines
And limped home dragging shattered screens.
How many were carried on stretchers

To be saved or dumped at a landfill.
How many were missiled into hundreds of pieces.
How many were buried in collapsed apartment
Buildings, left longing for sofas crowded with eyes open.

I pick up the remote and it rejects me,
No, reviles me, refusing to display channels
That are mostly still too wet and red,
The screens smeared beyond comprehension.

The remote is a gun firing blanks
As the door is being kicked down.
The remote demands that I keep
My hands raised above my head.

Trumpets of Jericho

Chicago traffic unmoving as the Lake Michigan skyline.
Main road through the city closed for the weekend:
bridge demolition. Detour leads through the congested west end.
Cars desperate for another way home as if this day was
different and not the usual detour to the unpromised land.
Streets crowded with older model cars racing
their engines, growling to get started, festooned
with strange flags tied to antennas, held out windows,
propped under windshield wipers, horns bleating
out the inconsolable rhythms of victory but nowhere
to go but around the block and back into the bar,
leaving the high-walled streets still standing
and congested with their cries.

The flags foreign, a red star on a black triangle trailing
blue and white bars. In the Windy City, more storms
forecast as we drive across another foreign land.
The radio wears itself out with the news of a second day
of tornadoes plowing up small towns in Nebraska.
There are so many of us that we can't get out of the way.
Even grave-deep shelters are only graves.
We can't get out of the way of ourselves
and the caterwauling winds blaring their trumpets
and cash in through the blades of wind generators.

Secular Circularity

His Grandfather, in a poker game, won his German
    grandmother from her brother
in one dark corner behind the stacked beer barrels in a
    Mainz warehouse in 1894.
Her last name was Grebb. Her grandson never liked her
    very much
she always greeted him, "Too soon *alt,* too late *schmart!"*
    At least, they left
Germany before there were any final solutions. Now he's
    selling his house
in a Chicago suburb where the local weekly paper
    headlined: *Snake Invasion*
Filling Basements. A little too much rain tipping the
    scales, keeping buyers away.
So he's on the Catholic Supply website learning about
    Joseph.

St. Joseph, husband of Mary and earthly Father of Jesus,
    the patron saint
of married couples, families, carpenters, and workingmen.
    Italian and Poles
said to be especially fond of St. Joseph with his special
    powers in real estate
transactions. Discovered by nuns who buried medallions
    with his likeness
on property they hoped to acquire for convents. Later,
    the medallions
were replaced with plastic statues and the focus changed

from buying

to selling. The statues are to be buried upside-down in
    the front yard

with the feet pointing to heaven. It may face toward
    the home

or towards the street if you want your neighbor's home
    to sell.

The statue location can vary: by the "For Sale" sign,

in a flower pot if you live in a condo, maybe on each
    side of the house

if you are in a hurry. Maybe even in pairs with head
    and feet pointed

in opposite directions, covering all the bases.

After the home is sold, the statues should be dug up,
    the dirt left

in the robe's plastic folds, and given a place of honor
    in the new home.

He's thinking about buying the Home Sales Kit that
    includes a 3.5 inch

plastic statue and laminated prayer card to be spoken as
    St. Joseph is buried

in the yard. He's buried thousands. But then there's also
    St. Joseph

the Worker's Home Sales Kit and the book, *St. Joseph,*
    My Real Estate

Agent and the gift-boxed Fontanini 4.5 inch resin
    St. Joseph statue

with the additional Home Sales Instructions.

When the Other Shoe Drops

A tire-flattened, laceless leather shoe that hasn't been worn
in months, its toe pointed away from the curb, perhaps
not ready for the next step into traffic with its promise
or threat of another thousand-mile journey; or maybe
nowhere to go without the thought of worth or gain.
End of this street, the congested intersection, the town's
loose limits, the earth more flat than ever as all destinations
are temporary. Lacquered box within cracked lacquered
box, each opening into a smaller room, so why work
so hard to get there rather than here, one step to close
the door from either side.

This postage-stamp lawn that fronts a busy street has no sense
of direction, can't cross the sidewalk or risk being run down
on this broad but short thoroughfare. Truck, diesel engine
knuckling up through its gears, jumps the curb,
the long-haul driver suffering an aortic aneurism,
parks itself beside the curbed leather shoe.
The driver walked off before the door can be opened,
a castaway, a two-bit player slumped over the steering
wheel in the cone of a street light, not even a chance
to bow to the grasses' green applause. Resignation is
as good a place to stop, rest, procrastinate, wait
for a single-shoed pedestrian to pass,
listen for the foot fall of a mirror-polished
patent leather never meant to be found
on the streets of Seattle or Madrid, predicted
by Heisenberg's Uncertainty Principle to coexist.

One Sixty-Fourth of Everything

A broom doesn't work.
A flyswatter won't work.
The mad buzzing bounces off every window.
No matter how quick he sweeps the air,
the dustpan too small for this quickly shifting
volume, the trash already too full of crumpled
notes, mostly the chaos of hemi-demi-semi-quivers,
like a cloud of tone-deaf gnats or the quotidian
sixty-four lists, each with the same single item,
each note clamoring to lead the chorus of chores,
insistent as cicadas bursting with a mad-sewing-
machine heat tattooed to every stitch of sweat.
The diabolical rising and falling rhythms of locusts
as they relentlessly leave saw kerfs in the grain
of air and time with no unified field theory in sight.

It's all too quick, casting in, casting off,
casting out, even a cast call, there's nothing
to be done but sing the damn song out of his head.
He knows something is happening
but he doesn't know what it is "Mr. Jones," except
for the time past and a tune that keeps rattling
around like beans in the mariachi of his skull.
A metronomic accounting: two flight-challenged
mourning doves' wobbly beat just above the telephone
wires that diagram the street and most of its holy shouts
and holier whispers. Four dump trucks can't
make up a direction so idle in no hurry
beside the curb waiting for a cardinal point
to be resurrected. Six flags over an awning

entrance that can't scrape up enough wind
to declare their flagging nationalities,
their only use to sell more imported beer.
Eight too-tall windows from another century
frame the unframed evening light, and he recalls,
sitting at the window near the bar, being consoled
knowing that he can't be alone or just alone.
Satisfied with the singular company,
recalling a friend saying, if he can't
be anything else be light: flashlight, floodlight,
search light, Kegel light, lighthouse, porch light—
warning that in a split-second the earnest search
is about to begin for another invasive song.

Porched

This terror and ecstasy of flesh begins on the porch.
The pitfalls of always leads to never, followed
By begging or nothing, for everything, down to the half-
Melted windows, their glass wavy ice cubes from
Drained gin and tonics.

Expired credit cards to purchase empty worlds,
Only to be on the lamb without bucolic pastures
To rundown, runout, to runaway, but today
The stalwart porch is the sinking bridge of a cruiser

Without the rhythmic roll of waves,
Without the whir of spinning radar towers,
No missiles primed for launch, no cannons
Loaded to fire, no shouts of panic, at least,

Not yet, no orders to prepare lifeboats,
It's just time to listen and listen some more,
The past has become dangerous, the waves
Towering and unpredictable, the ship

Changing its flagging colors with every turn,
Home port and port of call forever unknown.
Here in the shallows the oaks are drowning
in waves of last year's leaves.

Out the Window

All this dabbing just to fill the grain,
Flood the pores. A wide cheap brush
Fine for sealing beveled cedar siding.

Ladder a jumping off point,
And not a place to land, this walking
On rungs, as if the metal had grown dull

And the sharp ringing of each step belongs
To a life other than this one and everyone straining
To hear what's arriving through the humid air,

Always alert, always tense. The ladder with its own
Stiff stride, upright and vigilant, bobbing past
The window, a skeletal soldier on parade, proudly

Wearing the history of all its campaigns,
The white from too much priming,
The pastels of so many track houses,

The stains of the few who want to believe
They live outside and away from it all,
With a bucket that never goes dry

Even as it grows lighter and the level lower,
And still so much world to cover as the prophecies
Grow darker and rain bellies up to the hull of the house.

Home Crucifixion 1

Why did you ever think it was OK?
Well, the joke is already too tired
To toss another shovelful out
Into the ever-deepening hole of night.
The exhausted pause is necessary
Not to darken the drama
Though that's essential.
The pause is defensive,
The silence a barricade
As theories sharpen bayonets.

You've made it all the way home
with a mouthful of galvanized nails.
Swallow one and you will be nailed
from the inside out and not have to worry
about rust. In the house of words your tongue
Is a hammer. No one will be allowed
To escape. Who cares if there's a constant
Knocking. There are no doors. The rough
timbers are already crossed
and waiting along the road.

Home Crucifixion 2

The 16p through the sole of a left boot
And then up through the foot, missing
All the bones, so the sole is attached
To a 2 x 4 and the toes are wet and warm
Walking away from this small house of pain.

Then one that strangely left a parallel track
Down the inside of a young thigh,
Grip lost and slipping down
A porch railing in a nameless city,
Scars the only address left.

The one in the front of the knee
That tickled the bone but laughter was
Elsewhere, as if this were enough
Of a joke and in no further need of a punchline.

Holding on to what needed to be driven,
Pounded, straightened and hammered again—
Blackened blisters, blood-struck flesh,
The darkened moons of the mangled fingers,
The brute force that is always ready
To offer another hand.

Seven Seas

1 *Captain Ahab*
Months of turning pages of water,
of tired faces floating
in the hour's wake, desks adrift
in the debris of days,
students bobbing at windows.
Currents turn a few days
before school's end,
a concentration of flotsam and jetsam,
except for one boy,
trouble transferred from another
building, his legs dancing
to a sea chantey, his arms a tangle
of signaling semaphores.

2 *The Pequod*
The last days wash up
on sighted summer shores.
The release palpable
like a tsunami about to hit.
Students finally eager.
Work to complete.
Pages added to portfolios.
Crayoned pictures torn from walls.
Pencils, papers, photocopied
awards signed by the teacher,
stuffed into boxes.

Heads downturned, staring
into the pool of their desks,
holding their breaths.
They want to catch the ship
when it steams through
the double doors.

3 *From the Galley*
It's a served-up, end-of-the-year assignment.
A student hands in his paper,
The Poon Tang Pie Shop.
The teacher is upset.
She shows it to other teachers:
Is that a town in Louisiana?
I think it's Vietnamese.
Isn't that a diagnostic test?
I think I heard that in a Ted Nugent song.
How can she be sure?
She was just born knowing
what it is. She bets
another teacher
a pot of Italian soup
that the principal knows
what *poon tang* is.
The next morning
in the teachers lounge
bowls, spoons, soup.

Terry Allen

Terry Allen was born in Brisbane, Australia, grew up in Kanas City and is an emeritus professor of Theatre Arts at the University of Wisconsin-Eau Claire, where he taught acting, directing and playwriting. He is the author of four poetry collections: *Monsters in the Rain, Art Work, Waiting on the Last Train,* and *Rubber Time.* His poems have appeared in many journals, including *I-70 Review, Third Wednesday,* and *Popshot Quarterly.* In addition, his work has been nominated for an Eric Hoffer Book Award, a Best of the Net Award, and a Pushcart Prize. His books are available at Amazon, Kelsay Books, and locally at Skylark Bookshop in Columbia, Missouri.

The Rule of Three

Three elderly professors examine a large painting in
an art gallery.

There's the Holy Trinity of course.
Oh my, yes.
Omne trium perfectum.
It gives one pause just to think on it.

Friends, Romans and Countrymen.
Simple, appealing…
And effective.
We're pattern-seeking machines.
No doubt.
Oh yes.

Entertainment?
Hope, Crosby and Lamour.
Patty, Maxene and LaVerne.
Groucho, Harpo and Chico.
Larry, Curly and Moe.
Not to take things too lightly.
Oh no.

Some primitive cultures…
Yes?
Famously had only the numbers one, two and many.
Really?
Oh yes.

But why three oranges?

Ah! That's the great mystery.

Why not for instance…no oranges at all?

No oranges?

Yes.

You may have touched on something there.

Yes?

No oranges and yet the piece is titled "Interior with
Three Oranges."

Oh my.

The viewer would then need to…

Yes?

Have faith that the oranges are there nonetheless.

Hidden perhaps.

Out of view.

But notwithstanding…

They are present.

Just beyond the frame.

Out of reach.

Oh my.

Yes.

But what if nothing were outside the frame?

So, there is no outside?

The frame contains everything.

Everything visible perhaps?

Even the dark matter.

Composed of some as-yet undiscovered subatomic
particles.

Leaving us feeling a bit cold.

A bit out of place.

A bit unmoored.

Oh yes.

Old Windmill and Shed on Abandoned Farm
in Gray and Black

I recently saw a watercolor
in an art gallery of an old homestead
and I thought of Raymond,

my great uncle, who was one of ten
children, the one who never married,
who stayed on the family farm

near Oskaloosa and took care
of his invalid father, my grandfather,
who had fallen and broken his back

while patching a leaky roof...
my grandfather, who I only knew
in his later years when he was bedridden.

Raymond took care of him
and the farm and the chores and the house
with such fastidiousness that one of my aunts

told me, as if it was a great secret, "I'll tell you
something. That Raymond. You can eat
off his kitchen floor." That seemed odd to me

because I couldn't imagine
ever wanting to do such a thing, but
when my grandfather died, Raymond

scrubbed every inch of that house,
so people could eat off any surface
they wanted, I guess.

And then, as the family story goes,
he left through the kitchen door and walked
in the rain to the old gray shed out back

and rolled the log away from the plank door
and stepped inside to carefully
cover all the seed sacks and tools

with burlap, so as not to make a mess
before he knelt, as if in prayer,
and rested his chin on the double barrels

of a 1902 Davenport side by side shotgun
…and…that…as they say…
was that.

And for me, that was that,
until I later remembered having asked
Raymond about the name "Oskaloosa"

He told me that town lore said
the place was named after a Creek princess
who married a Seminole chief named Osceola.

and explained that tradition said her name
meant "last of the beautiful,"
but Raymond said that wasn't so.

"Oskaloosa" in the Creek
language means "black rain"
or "black water."

I liked his stories and today
when I think about it,
it seems that's all that's left...

except maybe somewhere
in an antique shop that features items
scavenged from old farm buildings

someone will find a weathered shed door
with rusty hinges and words scribble
on the inside that were once spoken

by a Seminole chief named Osceola:
"Let our last sleep
be in the graves of our native land!"

Waiting on the Last Train

An elderly couple dances in each other's arms.
He sings softly.

I'm the Sheik of Araby. Your love belongs to me.
What made you think of that?
It was used twice in the score of Fellini's *8 ½*.

Was it? I don't recall.
At night when you're asleep, into your tent I'll creep.
That sounds creepy, all right.
It was written in 1921.
Before my time.
It's in the public domain now and has become a jazz
    standard. Maybe I should record it.
In your dreams.
Aye, there's the rub.

Never mind your musical fantasies. How are you doing?
Most of my parts are working, I think.
That's good. How are your hips?
I like my right one better than my left.
You're still having pain?
A bit.

Do you think Guido killed himself in the end of the
    movie?
Possibly. Do you?
Well, he did crawl under the table and shoot himself in
    the head.

True. But he also escapes a traffic jam in the beginning
of the film by climbing out of the vehicle's window and
floating over rows of cars and ascending into the clouds.
That's Fellini's fantasy of escaping a stifling situation.
Maybe crawling under a table and shooting himself is
another fantasy about escape.
Maybe. But I like the ambiguity.

The stars that shine above, will light our way to love.
If you can't correct the problem, incorporate it, I guess.
You'll roam this land with me.
I know. *You're the Sheik of Araby.*
To the very end.
To the end.

About the Light

On fresh and salt water
built of wood
in the nineteenth century
then rebuilt
in the twentieth century
as a circular tower
of reinforced steel,

a lighthouse
guiding travelers to safety
and warning
of potential dangers
sits at the entrance
to the Black River
on Lake Michigan

where it waits and watches
in the twenty-first century
at the West End
of the South Pier
in South Haven,

a scenic location
where a nineteen-year-old
in a white t-shirt
and a black backpack
strolls by himself
to the end of the pier
and sits for a while

in a bit of shade
at the tower's base
watching the tall ships pass
before noticing
an elderly couple
holding hands
and looking out at the water.

He rises and approaches them
with a 9 mm pistol
in his right hand.

What are you doing?
the wife asks,
when he points the handgun at her.

Without saying a word,
without answering her question,
the young man
shoots her in the face

and shoots her husband dead
and turns and walks
toward the brilliant beach
at the other end of the pier,

stopping only to shoot himself
in an open carry state
known for its stunning lake shores
and beautiful sunsets
that take your breath away.

Flying Squirrels Can't Really Fly

For Larry (1947-2023)

Like carnival clowns
that aren't quite human,
that appear in the dark
then bounce about too quickly,
first here then there, a blur
of loss, of death and infection,
unpredictable, hard to pin down,
hard to hold in one's mind,

his brittle memories,
dry as cicada shells,
crumble away
in rolling sand storms
out of reach
beyond the doors
that can't be opened,
beyond the lines
that can't be crossed.

My brother lives in a warehouse
now, with a few square feet
to move about, and a bed,
and a lounge chair in which
to sit or sleep near others,
clutching dolls
or stuffed animals
in front of a muted TV
with almost familiar images
looking out at him
from the screen.

He has good days and bad days,
and sometimes he passes time
watching the squirrel chase
outside his window,
amused a bit to see their dance
as they leap into the air
from tree to tree,
with complete faith
that their world makes sense,
and they need no safety net
to catch them should they lose
their way and fall.

But other times, the worst days
of all are the good days,
for they are when he looks about
and realizes where he is,
even though he can't quite
recall how he got there.

His memories…
thin fragments…
of torn fabric,
or carnival clowns
trying too hard to please,
or squirrels defying
the law of gravity.

He's not sure which.

Aunt Gracie

The writer's name came up and someone said, *I've never liked him since the time I saw him at Once Upon a Crime…that mystery bookstore in Minneapolis. He was there promoting his new novel, and you could tell immediately, just looking at him, that he was a misogynist. He didn't even need to open his mouth.* And that's when my thoughts turned to memories of Grace Shields, our senior-high school, college-prep, English teacher. She had us writing paper after paper with the understanding that any three errors in spelling, punctuation, or grammar resulted in an automatic "F." And back then, she considered grammar and punctuation a science and content an art. She was tough, and she expected a lot, but God bless her, she gave us plenty of opportunity to fail, then learn from our failures. I remember that she would never tolerate the mixing up of second person with first person and would certainly expect that if we used a word like misogynist that we would know what it meant, and I could hear Mrs. Shields saying, *Misogyny comes from the Greek roots misein "to hate" and gynē "woman." Therefore, misogynist means someone who hates women, just as misandrist means someone who hates men.* We called her "Aunt Gracie," but never to her face, even though we considered it a form of endearment. And even today if I drive outside the white lines of grammar and begin a sentence with a conjunction or have fun with long run-on sentences spinning out like improvised jazz or play fast and loose with the Oxford comma, I can still look outside the window, going 70 mph, and see the lines that Aunt Gracie laid down.

Folktales in the Dark

The poet wrote about her father
and how he loved watching Westerns
and how she did not watch them,
and then she proved it by reporting
that all the women in the westerns
were saloon girls with big soft hair,
which is too bad, because if the poet
had occasionally settled into a comfy chair
with a cool drink and big bowl of popcorn
in the dark room beside her father,
she just might have seen some interesting,
sometimes quirky, sometimes powerful,
sometimes dangerous women
sneak out of the saloons
late at night or early in the morning
and jump on a horse and ride
out of town with the men,
who were off on some heroic
or outlawish adventure in the wild
parts of the great western frontier,

just like Ma (Jenny) Grier, a large,
strong, sadistic woman on horseback
who joins the mob out to lynch
the "would-be" rustlers
in *The Ox-Bow Incident,*
or like the fourteen-year-old girl,
Mattie Ross, in *True Grit* who sets out
to find the man who killed her father

with the aid of a U.S. Marshal
named Reuben J. "Rooster" Cogburn
or like Etta Place, a lifeline
and an accomplice to the outlaw duo
in *Butch Cassidy and the Sundance Kid,*
or Helen Ramírez, a business owner,
who puts men in their place,
and is of vital help to Marshall Will Kane
in *High Noon*, along with his wife,
Amy Fowler Kane, a devout Quaker
and pacifist whose bravery ends up
saving her husband's hide.

And woven deep into the fabric
of these westerns, a viewer
might also find the frontier women
who never entered a saloon,
women who had to shoot, build, heal,
teach, cook, sew, work the farm,
and deal with everyday
hardships for their families,
women like Emily Tetherow
in *Meek's Cutoff* who holds
a small group of settlers together
as they travel across the Oregon
high desert in 1845.

And sure, western movies
often play with the "Western myth"
and tell simplistic stories of cutout
characters placed in the foreground
of grand, monumental vistas,

while beautiful musicals scores
accent the relentless tension,
and sometimes these western films
are morality tales about standing up
for what is right, while some westerns
want to subvert the western tropes,
and the men and women come out
alive and whole, like people
we might recognize, if we care to look.

My Aunt and Uncle Drop By Our House
for a Visit in the 1950s

Aunt Wilma was my father's sister
and Uncle Bob was her husband,
a milkman who was going to night school
to become a chiropractor, which he did later
and immediately rejected all regular
medical treatments. So, when my aunt
fell down the stairs and injured her ankle,
he refused to let her take pain meds or see an M.D.,
but instead worked on it himself
until her ankle, her foot and her lower leg
turned black and swelled to twice its size.
She became completely crippled,
and finally went to a doctor and found out
that it was broken, but that hadn't happened yet
when they popped in for a visit sometime
in the mid-1950s, which was a time
when our living room was off limits
to my brother and me and was only used
to entertain guests.

And once my aunt and uncle were seated,
my mother asked if they'd like some coffee.
What kind of coffee? Aunt Wilma asked
as if that made a difference,
as if the coffee being offered
might not be the best freshly ground coffee
on the market.

We only have instant coffee, my mother said.

Oh no! my aunt and uncle replied,
sitting back even further in their seats,
looking as if my mother had asked
them to hold a poisonous snake.

Without a beat, my mother,
seeing the situation before her,
shifted gears and with a straight face
said, *we used to have our own
shaded coffee trees in the backyard,
and when the beans were bright red
the boys and I would pick them
 one by one and spread them out
in the hot sun to dry,
and that was followed by the hulling,
the polishing, the grinding,
the sorting, and the storing.
And then, of course, we would only brew
a single cup at a time.
But that finally became
just a little too work intensive for the boys,
and so we switched to instant.*

That was my mother for you,
a woman with a flair for the dramatic,
a woman who could tell great stories
and play all the parts herself.

And when my aunt and uncle
looked over to my brother and me
for conformation,

we nodded in agreement,
and I rubbed my right arm,
attempting to show how sore
it was from ranking the beans
for hours as they dried in the sun.

God, bless mother.
It's no wonder I went into theater
to find out how these magic
moments are done.

But in all honesty,
instant coffee at the time
did taste like shredded cardboard
that may have been stored somewhere
in a trash bin close to old coffee grounds.

"And May God Bless You... You Jerk!"

That was the last thing she said
as she made her dramatic exit
on a busy Saturday morning
down the aisle and out the door
of the chain restaurant
that pretended it served
good ol' country cookin',
leaving the elderly couple,
seated at a nearby table,
a bit perplexed and stunned.

For only a few minutes earlier,
the angry woman had rushed
the couple's table to apologize
over and over, again and again
in an endless diatribe,
heavy with layered sarcasm,
sounding as authentic and genuine
as a large glass of oat milk
served next to a heaping plate
of imitation crab.

And in her apology, the beet red
woman explained that her infant
grandson, who had been screaming
at 125 decibels, just between
the noise intensity of a pneumatic drill
and a jet plane taking off...
for three or four minutes

at the table behind the couple...
that her infant grandson has "issues"
and cannot control himself.

And because she just happened,
somehow, to overhear the couple
saying to each other that
the infant should be taken outside
to calm down, that she was sorry

that the couple's precious breakfast
had been disturbed, and they
had been bothered in the least,
which really was too small a word,
to describe what the rest of us saw

when all hell had broken loose
during the infant's nonstop meltdown
and the man at the table appeared frozen
for those three or four minutes
with a fork load of blueberry pancakes
somewhere between his plate
and his open mouth,
his eyes watering and his teeth
aching deep down into the bone,
while the woman across from him,
grimaced in pain, her hair standing
on end and her ears bleeding.

In fact, the only customers
that seemed undisturbed by it all,
were the four young adults at a nearby table

who were laughing and amusing themselves
by blowing paper straw wrappings
at each other and the two beefy guys
at different tables behind them
who were arguing with each other
about the outrageous state of politics
and public behavior.

The Old Man Schmoozes with the Guy Who Owns a Bar around the Corner

I like your sign over there.

Yeah, it's new. It's only been in that spot for ten years.

"Keep your trap shut! No politics! No religion! No filthy language!" What kinda dump is this?

The kind you frequent every day.

That reminds me. Did you see what happened to that squirrelly guy on the news?

What? What squirrelly guy?

You know, that squirrelly guy who used to wear a bow tie all the time and pretend he was one of the big boys.

Oh, the guy who never met a conspiracy theory he didn't like? Like about the ruling class of secretive reptiles that are controlling the world.

That's him. The guy who looks like he was bullied every day in school.

What about him?

Well, did you hear what his lawyer said?

What?

She said the decision to kick him off the network was the most catastrophic event in television history.

No way.

Yeah.

What about the space shuttle Challenger disaster?

Or the Munich Massacre at the 1972 Olympics?

Or when NBC canceled Baywatch after only one season?

Or Keeping Up with the Kardashians?

So, what do you think? It looks like you've got an opinion as usual.

Well, I tell you what that kinda lawyerly talk reminds me of.

What's that?

Those big wind-twisted Ponderosa pines they got out in Utah.

How's that?

I mean, those kinda lawyers grab hold of the facts and bend them and twist them like they're trying to screw the head off a chicken.

That's her job, isn't it?

That's what I'm saying. Plus, the fact that she doesn't know what the hell she's talking about.

What do you mean?

I mean, she has no knowledge of broadcasting history.

Really?

For me, an event that was far worse happened in 1955 when Pinky Lee, a little guy who just wanted to make people happy, collapsed on camera during a live TV show and because his whole shtick was his slapstick antics and comic dancing and rapid-fire jokes, the cameraman and the director thought his fall was an ad lib and part of his act and no one helped him while the "Peanut Gallery" of kids was encouraged to keep cheering and applauding.

So?

He coulda died right there, while the world laughed, which was really what his life was all about anyway, I guess.

I see. I get your point.

There are worse things than losing your so-called news platform that makes everyone miserable.

Yeah.

Add that to your sign.

Okay.

You know, your sign needs more positives and fewer negatives.

Like…

Like: "Be kind. Bring joy. Leave 'em laughing. Help carry the load." for God's sake.

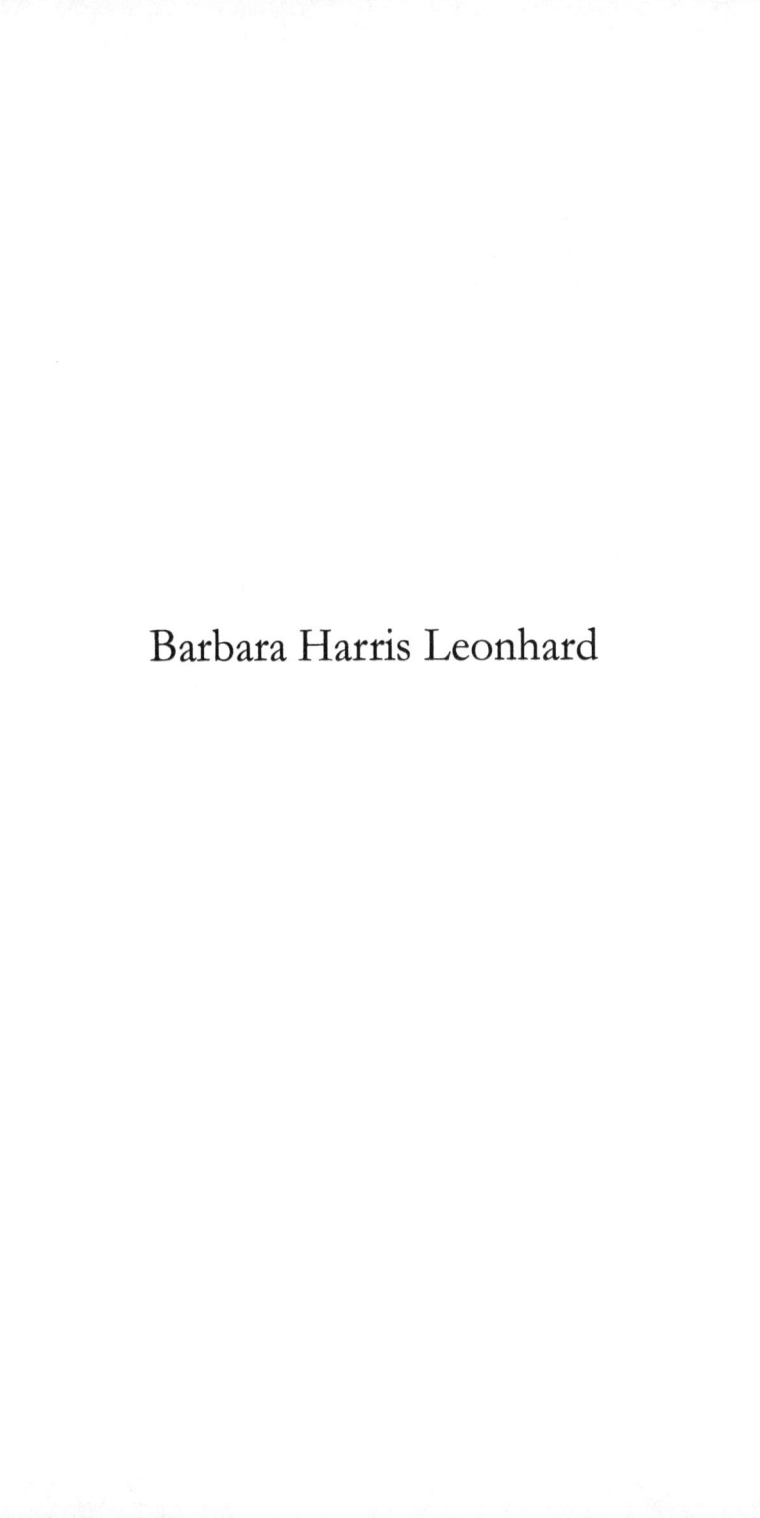

Barbara Harris Leonhard

Barbara Harris Leonhard's poetry has been published in various literary magazines and anthologies. She's also written a best-selling poetry collection *Three-Penny Memories: A Poetic Memoir* (Experiments in Fiction, 2022), which is about her relationship with her mother, who suffered from Alzheimer's. She has won honors from Spillwords Press and has been nominated twice for the Pushcart Prize. Trending Poets named her Poet of the Year 2023. Barbara is also the Editor for *MasticadoresUSA*. She lives in Mid-Missouri with her husband and cat Jasper, who refuses to take drives to Eagle Bluffs to count deer.

Surfing the White 'Cats': A Kayaker's Tale

The storm blows through.
I paddle upstream in the wind,
drafting the flow of the white caps –
You call them cats!

Wild enough as it is -
three-foot foamy waves -
I paddle farther and farther out into the river
to surf the biggest ones.

Beavers - two and a half feet long –
emerge from their holes.
An even bigger beaver,
three and a half feet long, I swear,
rushes into the water when our eyes meet.
No match for the six-foot-long
100-pound beaver I saw on a hike
when the river flooded.

Carp? Hundreds! One jumps.
Smacks me on my mouth.
Another clubs my shoulder.
When the river rises, crowds of carp
line up to graze on the grass at the riverbank
like cows at a feed lot.

On Perche Creek,
enormous schools of wiggling pencil fish
a foot and a half long each,
battling my paddle.

After a mile or two, dozens of vultures
roost on the dead tree
across from the landing,
where fishers pile gar and carp,
no effort to clean them –
just catch and dump.

Some fishers catch and release.
The bloody, torn mouths of the fish,
The slow deaths, the puffy bodies lapping
at the river's edge.

Today, the storm chases off the fishers.
I chase the wild white cats.

To My Knees, Whom I Named Tina and Cher

*Cher's reaction to Tina Turner's death, "...she gave me lots of
strength sometimes, and I gave her lots of strength, too. I think we
were perfect friends for each other, truthfully."*

My knees, Tina and Cher,
a well-aligned pair.
Talented and loved.
Both danced. Traveled.
Inspired each other on walks and talks.
Their stamina shone. But physical prowess
has an expiration date.
It swells with unresolved trauma.
Stabbing fears of falling off stages on the glory days.
"Shame, Shame, shame" on those who laugh
at the limp of a well-lived life.

On May 24, 2023, Cher and I lost Tina.
Cher rallied during Tina's decline
from osteoarthritis.
Both were strong for the new reality.
Good leg up and weak leg down.
Both knees cried stinging tears.
Both sported matching ace bandages.
Dragging on, exhausted as though holding up an anvil.
Prescribed workouts supported them.
Still, a surgeon replaced Tina
with a sleek, unnamed goddess.

Cher, we both grieve for Tina.
We three, once a team.
Now a new partner enters our triad.

We welcome this new angle—a pyramid again.
A symmetry restores us. With her
we can stand, drive, hike the river trails, bike for miles—
heck - we can even leap to the top shelf
with a single bound.

Aunt Rona Visits: I Forget to Mask

Gallows of Don't touch me
the haze of sneeze
I wring my clammy hands
run them over my scalp
snare hair to braid Rapunzel rope
to escape from the balcony
of a masked monastery
of lonely poems and bored stories
about breakfast in bed
My mistakes with air
I was promiscuous with smile
gulped arsenic lattes at Starbucks
like all was well and now
a case of everything in my belly
full of crushed butterflies
Choked bats hang in my throat in delirium
My lungs wheeze old bagpipe tunes
People run as I lock the gate.

Early Spring Snow

All is gray on our drive to the wetlands.
I shudder in the chill rising off the river.
A heavy fog huddles on the banks.
Tonight the sky stretches white,
as though the moon is seeking a view
from behind a lace veil. My lungs
are hollow in this air. I fear that snow
is on its way and will take the yard
and my route to the car. But I welcome
the buffering drifts, my hedge against an icy world
determined to plow you under. Scrape your vision dry.
The morning light will strike the shadows
into glistening mounds around the daffodils,
bowing to the weight of late winter weather,
smothering the boughs of the elm and pin oak.
Still, the birds will sing as though it's spring—
as though they're free.

Ophelia

There is a willow grows aslant a brook...
-Shakespeare, Hamlet

When the old willow weeps,
her shoulders bend to the sun,
her ancient songs resound
in tune with us

Her light binds us to her limbs

Her learning and duty, her strength
to stand firm as we battle

Her skirt, a shelter to our fallen

In her tears, no regrets
Our grief and despair seek solace
in this humble Sallow

We bow to her
in gratitude.

The Lost Child

I search for my embryonic dream,
lost too soon. Unable to hold on
in my misshaped womb.

A wolf leads me into a cave,
where I meet—Mark Twain!
He's dressed in white.
Has silver hair, like mine.

He regales me with his tales
of roughing it on the Big Muddy
as a steamboat pilot.

Though I love my walks and drives
along the Big Muddy, I know nothing
of the adventures and dangers
of reading rivers for safe voyages.

I stumbled into this cave
searching for help to find
my lost child.

He shares the loss of a brother, Henry,
to a steamboat boiler explosion.
He feels guilty about Henry's death,
failing to heed the warning in a dream.

I too have six siblings, not one gone—
except for the baby Mom lost as a teen.

A secret pregnancy. A tiny soul
who could have been an older sister.

Twain mourns his son, Langdon, taken
by diphtheria at 19 months
during a sorrowful and pathetic,
brief sojourn in Buffalo.

I still miss the little one I lost too soon
to be named and nurtured. It was
an abrupt ending to a dream.

He says that I do know the river.
Our lives share snags. We're strong vessels,
navigating tough currents, root wads, and rocks
that can tear our insides out.

Nothing that grieves us, he says,
can be called little.

The Found Poems of Amelia Earhart

Inspired by Traci Brimhall, "On Lost Lyric Poetry of Amelia Earhart: A Missing Pilot and Her Poems" (Literary Hub via New England Review, 02/01/2020)

Putnam guarded Amelia's lines

on death and desire

scribbled on envelopes

hidden in notebooks

No dates or context clues

Private flights of fancy

charred by a house fire

Metaphors jotted on pink notes, tiny sunsets

over a gray sea of scribbled graphite

Lyrics on women and beauty—images

splintered while plummeting

from the clouds, artifacts

half-buried in sand

somewhere

Blue Baby

In response to *"Woman Holding a Balance"*
- Johannes Vermeer (1664)

Mother of Pearl,
amorphous, warm sea.
Bearer of good tidings?
Protection, purity,
a polished life?

She carefully weighs the odds -
not just boy or girl, but survival
in a diseased world bereft
of love, bereaved of loss.

He strays and returns with gems
to soothe salty stares.

Strings of silky pearls
drape as lingerie, disrobe
a swelling chest.
Mystery fills the tough shell.

Blue jewel of lustrous nacre,
a summary of years,
a longsome anchor.

His apologies bare privilege,
laborious tenure.

No weight in the balance
of staying still
she considers

her blue baby.

His Mourning Heart

-In response to "Melancholie", a Statue created by Albert György in a park, Quai du Mont Blanc, in Lake Geneva, Switzerland

I see through my father
into his past, where he always lived,
where his joy burned
into embers of anger and loss
as though leaving the cottage by the lake
was as tormenting as his birth struggle
when he tossed and turned
to his mother's forced breathing,
the exit half-closed.

The forceps gripped his temples.
The extraction was his eviction from her
to the slap of cold light.
The late-life son clung to his crib,
suffering the fear of possibility.
Somehow, he survived
the stormy lake waves
and deep drifts of snow.

This is how he lived,
in struggle and doubt,
sensitive to harm,
to being pulled into caring
because caring was losing,
and losing was grieving.

This, a River

The river has great wisdom and whispers its secrets to the hearts of men.
- Mark Twain from "Life on the Mississippi" (1883)

My curves wind around sand bars,
creating islands revealed in low tide.
My arms form rivulets.
My legs flutter as waves,
creating the flow of time.

My current pulses life - tadpoles, carp, algae.
I smile in light, shimmering reflections.
I draw in birds to feed.
I am poetry for travelers on barges.
I hold kayaks as toys to capture in my eddies.

I can hold you,
can transport you,
can gather you into me,
into my dark, hungry fury,
your unexplored cosmos.

My age, Earth.
My creator, our mother.
I do her work, feeding her life,
dispersing bones and teeth,
treasures for children.

I shape Mother as she wishes.
I clean up her storms.

The overwhelming swells
of branches and trash
dissolve into me and my banks.

Her tears wash away our history,
revealing our present.

Mother's grief can nourish or drown.

This, a river,
cannot cry.

Lynne Jensen Lampe

Lynne Jensen Lampe edits academic writing, reads for *Tinderbox Poetry Journal*, and has recent poetry in *The Inflectionist Review*, *Rise Up Review*, *THRUSH*, *Figure 1*, and elsewhere. Her debut collection, *Talk Smack to a Hurricane* (Ice Floe Press, 2022), concerns motherhood, mental illness, and antisemitism. The book is a 2023 Eric Hoffer Award winner (honorable mention–poetry, grand prize shortlist) and a finalist for the 8th Annual McMath Award. Lynne lives in Columbia, Missouri, with her husband, two dogs, and a friendly number of dust bunnies. Visit her at https://lynnejensenlampe.com or https://linktr.ee/lynnejensenlampe for links to socials and poems.

Jitter and Shimmer

Maybe it means nothing, the pile of dead
bugs on the corner of my desk. I smash
another brown recluse with a wire cutter,
fingernail-flick dried flies into wings and legs.

Honky tonk on the stereo, second G&T half gone,
you're in the kitchen waiting. *Give me*
ten, I say, and step into the shower.
You are not young. I am not wise. We
are a shock of black-eyed susans wilting.

The box of love crickets you gave me
lies on the floor, lid askew. A branch moves
outside the window. Sunlight shafts
my bedroom and they sing.

The prescription on the plastic envelope reads
"Use 1 gram per vagina weekly." Lucky me!
I'll have enough for all *my vaginas*, I say.
Some women don't have any, you say.

We drink whiskey from plastic cups.
I ride along your thigh to the only music
that matters: the hum inside my jeans,
more power line than treble clef.
I am young. You have talent and curls.

Clouds clot a sky that only one of us sees.
I steal anger and tomato the shed. This not-me
pleasures in the spurt of pulp and seed,
readies for the next slap of rain.

No Sleep Is Safe in a Cold Bed

Missing him daggers my sleep
this sticky Missouri night.

A dream slurry claims me,
feeds me bayou, angry lover, young

doe limp and dying. A steep bridge,
the word *aliquot*, an old Fairlane

with its windows down, me
at the wheel, metal-cold. Empty

until he slides into our red bed
and his thighs wrap mine. I release

my carapace of worry to his heat.
The murk seeps into gardens

of hosta and coral bell, pokeweed,
sumac, black raspberry. Night warms

itself with our bodies, their tangle
of light waiting to rebuke the moon.

How to Change a Pillowcase

Day swells like kitchen trash
in a garbage strike. I fight
to open eyes crusted
with night, only to see sky

the color of furred tongue.
After weeks of nuzzling
my ex's pillow I'm tired
of breathing coconut & amber.

I snatch it from the bed,
hold the pillowcase at one end,
shield my heart & shake. Hard,
like a purse hiding cash, lipstick,
everything I've ever lost.
Strip the bed, then open

the closet to grab clean
sheets. See the dented box
of letters. Scour each one
for clues to what went wrong

& right. Wonder why a single
word—*cleave*—means both
securely attached & split in two.
Lug the laundry basket downstairs.

Forty minutes later I throw wet
tangles on the line. Lie on the grass,

imagine I'm at Discovery Park.
Hear waves shush against rock & sand.

Nestle into my own bare arm
& call that pillow good.

When Light Gardens for Truth

When the moon dresses like a man
who buries his life in pieces
at midnight, light cares nothing

for safety—it wants proof.
Alfred Hitchcock knew what he was
doing when he gave a man open

drapes & dead time, binocs to watch
light meander rooms in courtyard
apartments where occupants fear

fire without heat, fact without reason.
Shame without shadow.

Rear Window sends a message—leave
desire until the sun sheathes its rays
& daubs the dark with dry-grass

perfume. Everyone knows the moon
wears lies, clods of earth covering its satin casket.
Give light a shovel. Tell it to dig deep.

Never Stay Where Grief Is Free

Our breakfast at the shed—bottles of Bud Light
stand hip to hip along all four walls, empty.
Shame muscles past dirt-streaked glass, a fall
from grace, another truth for me to swallow
with fried egg and toast. Angry, you
ask for more of everything except wonder.

When we were fourteen, we visited World of Wonder,
a fenced lot somewhere in Texas—its spotlight
raked stars, erased constellations and you
yearned for a different summer, one empty
of friends and western diamondbacks that swallow
doves whole. Even now, you sleep where rivers fall

silent, where no other bodies break your fall.
You scrawl a message to me: *No wonder
solitude costs less than the Holiday Inn.* A swallow
of water from an old army canteen but no light
for a smoke—you dig around, come up empty,
add a postscript: *What if I can't lose you?*

•

Disappear: a transitive verb, fear its object. You
are not the young bodies left among deadfall.
I am not the parents who raise photos like empty
pockets of tears, yet I choke back wonder,
fear what will happen if you abandon your light
to the mourning dove and the swallow.

Grief is a country, its anthem a swallow
of vinegar and fear. Please let me sing you
beyond it borders once more until light
marries water, prison bends truth, hands fall
from hips unread. The night never wonders
what happens when the boulevards empty.

•

Years litter the shed, generations of empty—
an old Peterson's field guide marked at *swallow*,
the metal cot where Lulu birthed me, a wonder
of beer bottles. The creased snapshot of you
at the state fair after the swing-ride's fall
and spin stole your bravado. Even in this dim light

I see the vomit speckling your chin, the light-
ning urging us to shelter in an empty
car. Rain sings on the metal roof until nightfall
and no one missing us. Freedom swallows
the hours between backseat and home and you
show me the bruise on your thigh. I wonder

which fist inked this pain tattoo. I wonder
who else admires its yellow-blue light
and more than ever, I want to be you.
But dangerous is no better than empty,
not when envy sends its soldiers to swallow
resistance. I barely escape as footfalls

disrupt our river of bodies and tires. Offal
of love, ever dare me to wonder

if solitude costs less than solace. Bank swallows
burrow deep in the quarry wall. Moonlight
stitches my mother's apron into empty
sacks that shadow the shape of you.

•

Seeding clouds with doves and thunder, you
scissor both wrists on the first day of fall,
then call me before you run empty.
I rush to the shed, too late to stanch wonder,
floor and mattress stained red. Lost light
leaves nothing for the snake to swallow.

Wind whistles the bluff where swallows
dig nests, a colony of gunshots in sand. You
soul-slip as death pockets your tears, unlight
embroiders your name. Maple leaves free-fall
onto the tin roof, desert their steeples of wonder.
It's finally come time to empty.

Under the cot, a postcard of an empty
fairground, a field of bruises, a hard swallow
of time. Like the shed, a place of wonder
where layers of dirt bury memories of you.
Rain creases the clouds until nightfall
and cold wind begs to lease starlight.

•

No small wonder, grief: my body empty
of light, thirsty and calling freedom. I swallow
the song of you, sleep where rivers fall.

When Light Calls the City Home

Light hides in his fist and
stays, becoming something
else, four fingers and thumb
furled into a grenade

daring strangers to pull
the pin. As he strides the alley,
his fist holds shards
of night, remnants of stars,

refuses to be responsible
for the power coiled in muscle
and bone. A shudder and cough
open his hand. Light

floats from his flat palm,
becomes a dawn bruise of sky.
It casts yellow breath on brick
buildings and gingko trees,

sinks into the concrete
that lids the dark,
dissipates and doesn't care.
There's always another fist.

Love Language

I hold my mama's hand while we visit on the ward. Just
    this once
I won't worry about her Thorazine shuffle or the gray
    cotton

gown she wears. Just this once I listen to her stories of
    the other hospital
inmates, people I'll never bake cookies for or write into
    a poem. Just this

once I notice *trauma* rhymes with *mama,* but I won't tell
    how
she slugged the cop at the door when Daddy called 911
    for help.

Just this once I won't admire her ability—when she
    thought
her arms & legs were lost, scattered on the floor—to
    phone

friends & ask them to drive her to the psych unit at
    Parkland & also
call my daddy at work to tell him she wouldn't be home.
    Now

she rouses over paper-cup coffee & just this once she
    won't ask
about the black hole she sees every time I smile, a space
    plugged

years ago with a crown. As we talk I won't remember
    slamming a
putter against her right cheekbone when I was nine. I won't
    ask

myself why. Just this once I label it *accident* & won't wish
    she was
like other mothers. Just this once I feel my anger. Just
    this once

it's my job to save her.

No, not just once. Always.

Fat Quarters

1.
Daddy's sisters wore flour-sack
bloomers—their stepmother wore
silk undies, flags of luxury run up

on a clothesline. No orphan train
for Arnold's ten kids. After their mama died
he married again, thanks to the magazine

salesman who found Arnie a wife
in exchange for a subscription.
Ida, who'd birthed her own babies,

could fit on the back of his Harley
and sew clothes guaranteed to be
handed down several times over.

She saved her songs and few smiles
for blood kin. Arnie's boys and girls got
just a heavy hand, a bottom-stinger.

Ida wasn't yet the calico-aproned
thickset woman who doted
on grandkids, doled out treats

from a yellow cookie jar, the one
my Wisconsin cousins covet
but one of Daddy's sisters gave to me.

2.

Rain splatters my windshield.
Instead of seeing water
beading on glass I see the whole

of what's beyond, what's behind:
Girls in the calico dresses of St. Joseph's
Orphan Asylum trudge the median

of Florida Boulevard, one hand out
for change, the other waving
red roses at drivers caught at the light.

Baton Rouge still had orphans
in 1970, marked by the clothes
they wore. Even now

you can buy squares of Dream,
Promise, Grace, Family. Hope.
The textile maker calls the fabric

Orphan Train of Memories—tiny
dots, daisies, and roses bloom
into quilts to make a place home.

Rough-Cut Elegy

1.

Fridays mean rye whiskey, a joint, a band
at the Corner Pocket. This time
I finagle a way home with the lead guitarist.
Next morning at Carleen's, I preen

when a guy in a booth—Brad, who runs
lights for the band—clocks our damp
hair, smirks at our hookup, waves
us over to his table. He wants to talk

color gels and set lists. I tune out, order
coffee and a short stack. Brad can shoot
the shit about anything—Song of Songs,
prime numbers, how to win Heroes

of Might and Magic. Fission
versus fusion. Paint solvents. He paints
trim for cash, spends what he has
on weed, liquor, a university library card.

2.

Fast-forward fifteen years. I'm back in town
after a decade in Seattle and engaged
to the lead guitarist. Brad and his bell bottoms
move into our curb-worthy RV, his alarm clock

wedged between Karkov vodka and Kierkegaard.
He babysits, shares groceries, shows up
drunk, smelling of turpentine and toe jam,
looking like he's tumbled dry and stayed

in the basket too long. One night he opens
his hunting knife in our house,
cleans a sharp blade already clean.
Tells us he plans to kill his stepmother

with that knife, then pounds our door
with a baseball bat after we warn her
daughters. We sleep with a machete
under our dresser and tell him to forget

the wedding. A month later he turns up
on a stranger's porch—black eye, swollen
jaw, heart attack. Dies at the hospital. Leaves us
tussling with God and the words to *Amazing Grace*.

When Light Unlocks the Cellar of Time

Anoint the days before illness, before absence,
before before. Femur & pelvic bone
clad in salt skin & shallow wounds
disrupt our resurrection.

Exhumed, bathed in lavender, vinegar, thyme—
furrow of death, fragrant
grief. We candle-wax hope. Paraffin
hollows & seals & hope always lights

its own match. Walls melt, pool,
jellyfish into corners. Lucent tentacles
kite an ocean of old toys & sorrow
larded with all the stingers

mothers utter in mother tongues.
Nailed to the church door, this
ode to a paper trail: birth record, W-2,
prescription pad, crematorium receipt—

quasi proof of a life. Memory drifts
rumble strips & center lines, sets its
sundial in the dark.
Taxidermists stuff seasons—time-trophies

ululate despite a moon missing from this
vault of despair. Bone scraper,
wield your blade and bare the truth.
X-ray vision lets us clock the scale of

yesterday's mistakes. Tomorrow we'll
zest the skin of chance.

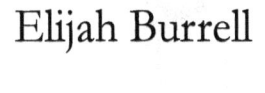
Elijah Burrell

Elijah Burrell is the author of the poetry collections
Skies of Blur (EastOver Press, 2024), *TROUBLER*
(Aldrich Press, 2018), and *The Skin of the River* (Aldrich
Press, 2014). In 2010, Burrell received the Jane Kenyon
Scholarship at Bennington College, where he earned
his MFA in Writing and Literature at Bennington's
Writing Seminars. He was awarded the Claudia Emerson
Scholarship from the Sewanee Writers' Conference
in 2019. His writing has appeared in publications such
as *AGNI*, *The Hopkins Review*, *North American Review*,
Southwest Review, *The Rumpus*, *Sugar House Review*, and
Measure. In 2012, Burrell joined the faculty of Lincoln
University, where he serves as Professor of English. In
2023, he received the Missouri Governor's Award for
Excellence in Education.

Dreamers and Drifters

Let everything with breath pluck strings,
shake tambourines, smash teacups
into sinks, and sing for ruined things.

Wandering Off

The quarter horse strides through the switchgrass
toward my father. He slides the bit into its mouth.
Its tail sways as he sets the saddle blanket
on its back in the late sunlight.
The horse's neck bows toward him,
and he stares as if he can almost see himself
in its dark eye. My mother tells him something,
or perhaps her gentle voice is directed to the horse.
Her small hand skims its cheek
as she speaks. He crouches down
to give her a leg up, and looks to her
with incredible patience.
We watch her ride across the field and dissolve.

My eyes open on metallic wallpaper
next to the hotel-room bed. A thin sheet
of light beams from the space between the curtains
that don't quite fit together. I look down
at the floor, the graveyard
of pillows, and stare at my lone reflection
in the television screen.

Favored

for Polly

West of the house, pink glory in the sky.

The honeybells hope for the hose.

The hummers buzz above for their last swigs of daylight.

In this moment, there exists no other place on earth.

Beside me, she sips the drink I prepared.

She floats through the pages of the book she's chosen.

With each small breeze, she tucks back strands of hair.

The small, solitary oak in the pasture

shines through the haze.

Her love for me is a mystery.

It astonishes.

It is undeserved.

It is miraculous.

Heartbreak Neophyte

My thirteenth summer, I worked beside my dad.
The lady from the warehouse office, the third affair,
the one I envisioned long after my bedtime
beneath hot covers, would every so often catch
a ride home with us. Her house was on the way.

The inconvenient son, I closed my eyes
and made believe I slept in the backseat
minutes before she asked,
   You think he's asleep?
   When can I see you again?
I hope it's soon, he said, with classic country
meandering from the AM station.

I stirred when she slid from our car and waved goodbye.
   Do you love her? I said.
His glimpse, brisk.
You misheard, he said, and turned.

That evening, I left the dinner table early.
My mouth never opened: a cocked gun, unused.
I listened to his favorite station in my darkening room.
The model starships and airplanes, hung by fish line
above my bed, pitched left to right from the vent's
fresh blast and dimmed. A room over, the quiet
dispute washed out as the music converted me
into a heartbreak neophyte. Two hours
I took in country songs he'd learned as a boy
and I'd heard in his car.

I imagined him lying next to my sleeping mother,
scheming escape, staring through their textured ceiling.
I heard the floor creak when he got out of bed.
Maybe his ears caught runaway notes, maybe
he wanted to talk regret with somebody.

He knocked on my locked door. He rattled the handle.

I didn't answer. I made believe I slept.
I wish I had answered. I made believe I slept.
I'm sure he heard the bull fiddle, the banjo, the mandolin,
but I didn't answer. I made believe I slept.

Where Have You Been

The snow falls like bright cotton
sheets swell and ripple
on clotheslines across
the America found deep
inside us.

It moves like a dress resuscitated
by wind, swirling piano-white-spread, fingered
in wet air—the one I slid down
her shoulders once
or twice.

The kids throw on their boots, the mothers
pull out their phones to post pictures of the
first snow. Flakes fall on our heads, float in the air,
like unexpected company. Like the ones
we've missed.

Reverberations

One day, I heard the neighbor boys make war.
I recognized the sounds. One yelled, *I got you—you're dead.*
The other shrieked from the ghost bullet, chest blown open.

That's not how it sounds when someone dies, the first boy yelled.
Once I called her number and let it ring for the voicemail,
but reached a number that had been disconnected or was

no longer in service. There are so many ways to hear it.
A robin flies away from its nest, disappears
into sunlight. That quiet. Today, it's exactly that quiet.

But last night I sat on the back porch and listened
to the newborn calf bellow from its hutch
across the pasture. From the far darkness, its mother
called out. From the far darkness, its mother.

When He Types Her Name It Autocorrects to Distant

One can
allow things
left unsaid and hanging
on the vine to ripen,
soft-sweet for later
tasting,
or
rot on the ground
to be stepped over,
forgotten, returned
to the cold places
from which they grew.

By This Pond

By this pond, where I slowly adapt to me without,
where I gradually get the fact I'm half a shape,
where I remember what it's like to crave,

and where I cast a line and watch it fall
closer each time to its imagined target,
delighting in the gear-spin of the handle.

This speed will catch the fish's eye,
this speed impersonates the thing the fish wants most.

I brought my friend to this pond, and he said it was hell
waiting for a fish to bite. I told him
the heaven is in that hell. He didn't get it.

A jolt, and my rod bends to the water, its tip
almost submerged. In the air one half stretches
to meet its rippling reflection on the water.
This shape, I know it now. Only in being
bent, does the heart become the heart it's meant to.

Diver\Down

At the local pool, he begged
his father to time him
as he gripped the coping and held tight
his breath beneath.
Sometimes he'd sink through
lukewarm bathwater
and stare at the light fixture above
as he practiced holding it in.
Silence, save the sounds his body
made: the throat squeaks,
his lungs burning to burst. Then the ceiling,
or the bright sun, or his mother's smile,
shimmered beyond the sky of surface.

Postlude / Grace

This morning, my daughter sat on the floor by the couch
as I played something indistinct on the guitar.
I passed it to her, and watched her miraculous fingers
move down the neck like a surgeon closing a wound
that's lain open too long.

Anand Prahlad

Anand Prahlad is the author of three books of poetry, *Hear My Story and Other Poems*, *As Good As Mango*, and *Dreaming of Endangered Species*; a memoir, *The Secret Life of A Black Aspie;* several critical studies on African American folklore, including *Reggae Wisdom: Proverbs in Jamaican Music*; and he has edited of two folklore encyclopedias, including *The Greenwood Encyclopedia of African American Folklore*. His poems and essays have appeared in many literary, scholarly, and disability journals. Prahlad is also a songwriter and musician, whose music spans blues, folk, and reggae, and he has released one CD, titled *Hover Near*, and is working on a soon-to-be-released CD titled, *Paradise*. He lives in Columbia, Missouri, and is a professor Emeritus at the University of Missouri, and an affiliate faculty at the Thompson Center for Autism and Neurodevelopment.

Twilight in Hanover County, 1965

In the silence that fell over the county
once we could sit at counters
you could hear a pin drop.

You could hear Chip's mama saying
you better leave them white girls alone.
You could hear his heart

thumping when he tiptoed through
the woods to meet Ginny.
You could hear the owls, the back seat,

someone crying out for Jesus.
When Chip got home, late again
it was like us walking into a white diner.

You could hear footsteps, water
dripping in the sink, forks shuffle,
everyone looking down at their plates.

You could hear Ginny's mom,
through crickets, cursing and sighing
to the cabinets. You could hear her

sifting salt on the roast.
When Ginny came, she tried to speak, but
the silence kept on ringing.

Shells

My granny is inside a robin's egg,
                shell blue as the shine on shoe tips
                    the ocean
                    off Monserrat

a 1961 Plymouth Valiant,
                the old-fashioned Pan Am
                    stewardess
                    jackets

the sky over mountain peaks in Nepal
                the petals of lobelias
                    hortensias
                    or Neptune.

*

My mother is inside a hawk's egg,
                on a high cliff above
                    flood waters
                    broken dams

blue keloids of her mastectomy
                gibbous bulbs on black
                    plain, porous
                    and tender

skin beneath prosthetic lithograph
                of remembered light
                    fragments
                    filaments.

*

I am inside a swallow's egg
        a nest of red dyes
             pesticides
             in shell shock

my bones beds of once-pink coral
        tongue-less humming birds
             pulse, throbbing
             capsicum

joints that groan and split conjoined
        to bright plum
             heavy limbs
             of stars.

sister

she would throw a broken tongue fix
on any tongue that dared to mouth me.

if bullies on the playground bothered me
she would break their bones.

she would hold the umbrella
and shape my hips with hopscotch

and take my belts and scars and be
the mouth that was often smacked.

sister was the closest thing
i ever had to a shadow.

she fought them so hard that night
they took me to the Greyhound.

she bit and shrieked aloud when brightness
in the station singed my eyes

and turned my skin to pustules.
she spat at anyone who stared.

i watched them through a window
smeared with lipstick and handprints,

with impressions of someone's cracked
forehead, and rocked and tapped

my fingers like a blues man,
like a patient in a padded cell

pounding on the wall, all the way
to some place in Philadelphia.

Creation

1

I would keep her company
            when daddy was never home
and the purple value of damson rose
            like flames, burning across acres
of orchards and gardens,
            when the blues gave way to gospels,
gold robes behind the pulpit
            swaying reeds of Bethany
Baptist and the black dancing
            scream torn from a sinner's
throat. I would be the tear drop
            of the blessed savior
as she lightly rubbed her palms
            across the thin membrane
of belly skin, slowly up and down
            imparting need to supple bone
tissue, forgiving organs, cells
            blossoming like magnolias
and I would shift in water
            to the touch of singing, weep
the melody of longing, become
            an opal thud, thing pushing.

2

But when I came I came like the Lord's fury,
            like one of the Lord's biblical plagues.
I came like the wind upturning rooves.

I came like the sorrow of lost worlds.
I came with one arm missing
        and a bird singing in my pubic bone
and a cavern in my baby bald nest.
        And like a storm I flung them across the room
and pinned them against the banister and walls.
        I covered the house with rain that rose
like fog, with light their bitterness couldn't touch,
        their hatefulness, shame and embarrassment.
Day after day as they seldom fed me, hardly
        changed me or picked me up. Night after night
as they sat spellbound in black and white in front
        of the television, while I grew gills to breath
beneath the surface of my aloneness, fins
        to swim into the currents and depths of plant
breaths, and slowly turned the house into a sea
        where I could feed on chlorophyll, to take
the edges off my hunger, still, I nearly starved.

Mana

I am myself
speech of no speech,
music of the flute
cats and dogs hear.

Through the eyes of flesh,
phospherous
and sulfer gut
I came into this world.

The molecules of fog,
fir in the forest,
nose to nose on ground
with particles of flame.

Spoken by no tongue,
mangled by no finger
or lied into concrete breath
for no bloodlust or money.

I am myself
the dance of no movement
sunrise on the desert
of a different planet.

This. Washing
without any water.
Living without hunger
dying without thirst.

This. Falling
never to break,
trees by the river
stars understand.

The Cows

A listening animal, like a cow
will hear your shadows
coming across the field.
Will see the shadows of tree limbs
and willow leaves
walking and talking like men
descending mountains,
being chased by revenants
and haunted by the decimals
            of their lives, who
for a minute were determined
to come home,
but woke up along the way
and couldn't remember
where they were going.

A listening animal, like a cow
will shiver from
the instability of shade,
from the slowly shifting
of tenses
            spread out by oaks.
From the deep red weight
of hens clucking in the barn,

the trebling stench of camphor

and manure, beast

sweat and straw.

From the moon

 over fences, and the shadows

of slave spirits plowing

without plows, drinking

        without water,

aging without time,

weary of waiting

and about

        to enter

another embryo and once again

start dreaming.

Helium

From the shadows of a brown recliner
he's sunken in, like a cavity,
a germ that will cure cancer

his body lifts like helium
and he descends on her like a cloud.

You remind me of the modernists,
she says, thinking aloud,
in the single moment of clarity

before drug film fogs
her thoughts, and the gown
she's in, and the bars screening

light seem to come closer-
and the modernists are like

the cigarettes after. The mints.
The corroded edges of wishing
to be something more than you are.

She remembers promises she made
to herself. She remembers
they're out of time.

She remembers the long distance
between patient and her name,

to hold her breath
and pretend she's nothing but water.

Remembering San Francisco

Those years when the tar of coke or sweet
marijuana resin and patchouli
oozing from your skin is like the scent
of night jasmine exploding
along the sidewalks of the avenues.
When you try so hard to enter one place
without leaving behind the other,
or better, you try to get dressed
without first taking off your clothes.
Those years when you thought that walking
down an aisle, bowing and being hooded
would make the ghosts disappear,
would make the seas magically part.
You would ride a clean train to work
and eat Reubens on rye in a café.
You would strut down a busy street
or stroll across a campus where the lawns
were more pampered than most
of the world's children.
But the years would pass,
like barges on the bay. Day after day
the voices would take shape,
glimmering like sad shadows.
They would press the bell on buses
and on street cars. They would
follow you off and take you into alleys
and leave you, looking for things
you could never remember.
Just to lie down and get up.

Just to say yes to morning
would take all day. And then there'd
be the lost nights at Denny's
peering into drained cups, waiting
for stray grounds to reassemble
into sentences you could go to bed with.
Peering out into a dark lit by bodies
on fire, by neons over the homeless
and bright fishnets and flashing red cop lights
and the lime green hats of pimps.
Another night under elms in the park,
near a small herd of buffalo.
You could hear the winos gagging and
laughing over in the next valley.
Your body balled into a shivering fist
and the wet breath of plants
on your cold, dirty skin. Then, nothing,
for a long time, but never long enough
before the loud crows would rip it open.
Before the wind would bring faint
scents of juniper and diesel. Before
you would rise to another morning of mist,
of light swelling over the eucalyptuses,
over the firs, as the distant sounds of
tires on the freeway would surge
though heavy, cypress air, intangible
as the fading memory of a kiss.

Adrift

We were like the earth before the continents
once, before pieces of land separated.

Each thing was felt, or at least it seemed
by every other thing.

If an acorn fell in the eastern forest
it rippled in the western hemisphere.

When the moon paused over a northern village
the clock stopped in all directions.

But that was before I lost a year's length
of pink colon bent on unraveling, a prostate
riddled with tears of sea salt, so much sand
slipping through numbed fingers.

That was before the caravan of surgeries
whose echoes never seemed to end
and I fell forward into a darkness
that covered me in all directions.

We waited for the distillation to come.
For the alchemy of pain turning
into memories.
We entered the willing suspension

of disbelief as we would a bomb
shelter. As we had the rhetoric of hope

watching coral reefs disappear
and glaciers turning into warm waters.

Something was lost besides flesh
and weight with all
the uncontained belching and gurgling,

perpetual bleach white on cold porcelain,
wet pajamas and sheets, wet
chairs, sofas, and ruined suits.

We became two south poles of the magnets,
one desperate, the other, even in the face
of histories and momentums
awash, repulsed.

I love you was still a sugar plum
but we couldn't taste it.

I could dream of it, but only through the haze
of opiates, cocktails, the weekly sacrifice
lying still barely covered

and feeling as stuck in place as a monarch
needled between the pages of a book

somehow
I could never arrive at grace.

At night in bed, foghorns in our breaths
and light houses in lonely bones
spilling an unblessed darkness across
shorelines and currents

denying safe homecomings
or passage,

two bodies with so much time and space
and in between so much blue water.

Patching

The neighbors patch things together
with chickens. A new dog.
Turning red brick feudal with coats
of limewash and greyed tint.
Sudden home gardens and raised beds.
Tomato, sweet pea and blackberries.
I mostly sit and watch. Listen.
My wife's turning the doorknob.
The garage door lifting and the quiet
Prius engine coming and going.
I know the wind whistling through
the top floors of trees is not to be missed.
Nor the glimpses of green, of early
grapes through slotted spaces
of lattice. Are there certain people
whose bodies hold no Rosetta stones,
no maps or keys that, when you touch
or look at them, will ever help them
to make sense? I grow luminous
with age, but not so much with light.
I have no clue to how to patch
things together.

This project was made possible, in part, by generous support from the Osage Arts Community.

Osage Arts Community provides temporary time, space and support for the creation of new artistic works in a retreat format, serving creative people of all kinds — visual artists, composers, poets, fiction and nonfiction writers. Located on a 152-acre farm in an isolated rural mountainside setting in Central Missouri and bordered by ¾ of a mile of the Gasconade River, OAC provides residencies to those working alone, as well as welcoming collaborative teams, offering living space and workspace in a country environment to emerging and mid-career artists. For more information, visit us at www.osageac.org

Osage Arts Community